Ethics in Victim Services

Ethics in Victim Services

Melissa Hook

Foreword by
Edwin Meese III

Sidran Institute Press
Baltimore, Maryland
and
Victims' Assistance Legal Organization
McLean, Virginia

Library of Congress Cataloging-in-Publication Data

Hook, Melissa, 1951–
    Ethics in victim services / by Melissa Hook ; with a foreword by Edwin Meese III.
    p. cm.
    Includes bibliographical references and index.
    ISBN 1-886968-17-9 (pbk. : alk. paper)
    1. Victims of crimes—Services for—United States. 2. Victims of crimes—Legal status, laws, etc.—United States. 3. Social workers—Professional ethics—United States. I. Title.

HV6250.3.U5H66 2005
174'.936288—dc22

2005009936

This project was supported by Grant Number 95-MU-GX-K002(S-7) awarded by the Office for Victims of Crime, Office of Justice Programs, U.S. Department of Justice. The Assistant Attorney General, Office of Justice Programs, coordinates the activities of the following program offices and bureaus: Bureau of Justice Assistance, Bureau of Justice Statistics, National Institute of Justice, Office of Juvenile Justice and Delinquency Prevention, and the Office for Victims of Crime. The opinions, findings, and conclusions expressed in this document are those of the authors and do not necessarily represent the official position or policies of the U.S. Department of Justice.

Contents

Foreword

Edwin Meese III
Attorney General of the United States (1985–88)

The crime victim assistance movement has developed over three decades, led by a number of pioneers: insightful criminal justice professionals, committed public officials, dedicated workers serving victims, and crime victims themselves. The latter group was a driving force in charting the early path of the movement, as victims expanded public knowledge of how the dramatic and devastating effect of crime had changed their lives. This led to a significant transformation in how our nation views crime victims and responds to their needs and concerns.

In proclaiming the first National Crime Victims' Rights Week in 1981, one of these pioneers, President Ronald Reagan, said:

> We need a renewed emphasis on, and an enhanced sensitivity to, the rights of victims. These rights should be a central concern of those who participate in the criminal justice system, and it is time all of us paid greater heed to the plight of victims.

I have had the good fortune to observe the progress that has been made as America, indeed, "paid greater heed to the plight of victims," and to participate in the field of crime victim assistance that emerged from the initial stage of dedicated grassroots organizations to the strong, dynamic, and dedicated profession that exists today. I have watched the growing pains as those in the field struggled to obtain laws that define and protect victims' rights, sought funding for basic, essential services to help survivors of crime cope with the trauma of victimization, and worked in communities across the nation to educate people in America about what it means to be a crime victim.

New challenges have arisen along with this tremendous growth and development. Today we must ensure that the laws that are enacted and the services we provide for victims are based upon their most salient needs. We must work together in cooperation with justice officials, policymakers, health and mental health professionals, social service workers, the faith community, victim advocates, and others to identify and effectively meet the needs of a wide range of victims. We need to provide seamless services that leave no victim behind. Perhaps most significantly, the victim assistance discipline must establish and hold itself accountable to the highest standards of service, leadership, and ethics.

The emergence of the victim assistance field as a profession should not negate its origins as a powerful social movement in America—one that has resulted in the establishment of over 10,000 victim assistance programs and over 33,000 victims' rights laws at the federal, state, and local levels. Today the profession of victim assistance continues and reflects the struggles of the early pioneers. They created programs, policies, and practices that were victim-centered, and that recognized each person who was victimized was an individual deserving of compassion, respect, and assistance. This high standard holds today and must continue to hold in the future.

When I think of high standards in leadership and ethics, I think of my good friend Frank Carrington, Esq., who founded the Victims' Assistance Legal Organization (VALOR) and is considered to be "the father of the victims' rights movement." Frank gave his heart and soul to legal advocacy and assistance for crime victims. He was truly a pioneer whose vision shaped the early grassroots victims' movement and planted many seeds that grew into the full-fledged profession of today. Frank's untimely death in 1992 was a devastating blow to the field of victim assistance.

On January 22, 1992, my colleague Donald Baldwin, among others, paid tribute to Frank Carrington in the U.S. House of Representatives:

> Frank touched the lives of thousands of people: those
> with the highest levels of accomplishments as well as

those who had no resources of any kind, but whose causes were desperate and whose needs were great.

He was never too busy. He was never too over-worked; at least, that was the impression he gave to those who called him for advice and counsel . . . both professional and personal.

He was a good man, kind, and considerate of everyone. Frank epitomized what our Lord tells us about real compassion—that true caring for people involves more than just words or feelings. It involves action.

The standards of excellence, compassion, and commitment described by Mr. Baldwin are the ethical foundation for the victim assistance movement. If victim assistance workers challenge themselves and their profession to meet such standards, they will honor the vision and heroism of Frank Carrington. This book, developed and written by Frank's successors at VALOR, with the support of the Office for Victims of Crime, is a fitting tribute to him and his dream—that crime victims would take their rightful place in America's justice system and that their needs would be met with comprehensive and professional care that is compassionate, respectful, competent, and, in every sense of the word, ethical.

Preface

When the Victim Assistance Legal Organization (VALOR) began work on this ethics text a few years ago, several states and at least one national organization had already developed basic codes of professional ethics for their memberships. An implementation guide on ethical decision-making seemed like a timely contribution to the field of victim assistance, and I embarked upon this project envisioning the simple task of taking several agreed-upon ethical concepts and making them practical and accessible to the field.

As is generally my approach when I begin a project, I called upon advocates and direct service providers to share their experiences in the field. I asked them to tell me about the kinds of ethical dilemmas they face in their work with crime victims. Their feedback has been immensely valuable in developing realistic content for the text and their stories appear as case scenarios throughout. However, I also learned that in the field of victim assistance, a standardized code of professional ethics is a "hard sell" because it is tied up with differences over professional credentialing, turf issues, and disagreements over what constitutes ethical priorities.

I reconsidered my approach more than once before I settled on my objectives for the text. My goal is to make practical what is theoretical, but I also want to shed light on areas of controversy and to encourage exchange among service providers with sometimes competing duties. Therefore, I define professionalism broadly—as the pursuit of excellence—without linking it to credentialing, and I define professional ethics as the code that supports the highest possible standard of service for crime victims. I recognize and respect the fact that community- and system-based organizations serve crime victims differently and are subject to different ethical priorities. I explore not only the practical application of ethics in the field but also discuss common barriers to ethical decision-making and inherent conflicts in the process. Whenever possible, I convey information through example and I do not expect that every reader will agree with my perspective or my proposed outcomes to sample ethical dilemmas.

Like role play, tools that offer us the opportunity to think through and discuss the "what-ifs" of our responses to ethical dilemmas present rich opportunities for discussion. In the process of writing this book, I never entered into a dialogue on ethics with my peers that I did not encounter passionate enthusiasm for the subject matter. When victim assistance providers can remove the "judgment factor" or the rightness or wrongness of the response from the discussion of ethical responsibility and view ethical dilemmas as problems to be solved, they will find that the fertile ground for communication among service providers on this subject grows significantly. What I really want to do with this text is invite victim service providers to join the discussion of how ethics can positively impact quality of services to crime victims. In that sense, I think of this text as a living document that over time will evolve and change based on feedback from our experts in the field, the service providers who have dedicated their lives to helping crime victims.

Acknowledgments

First of all, I want to thank Morna Murray who has been an invaluable contributor, reader and legal advisor on this project. A huge thank you to the many victim assistance providers in the field who have shared with me the ethical challenges they have experienced. Among those who helped at the initial stages of the project by making constructive suggestions are Jeanette Adkins, Sharon English, Carroll Ellis, Janice Harris Lord, Marti Kovener, Dana DeHart, Jane Nady Sigmon, and the folks at WIN Victim Services and Pennsylvania Coalition Against Rape. I want to thank Elizabeth Peterson for her thoughtful editing. I would like to thank Barb Paradiso, Anne Seymour, Trisha Gentle, Ana Soler, and Carroll Ellis for their careful reading of the final draft and their helpful comments. For their support and patience throughout the project I would like to thank Carolyn Hightower and Laura Ivkovich at the Office for Victims of Crime.

Introduction

This text provides an opportunity for victim assistance providers to bridge the gap between the abstract concepts represented in a code of ethical standards and practical work with crime victims. It seeks to connect the core values of the field with the commonly agreed upon ethical principles that support them, and then position the ethical standards in a real-world context. Too often, study of ethics occurs in an intellectual vacuum, where standards are discussed but the ease of their practical application is taken for granted. Then a complex situation arises where the standard is jeopardized and ethical response becomes a challenge.

Ethical decision-making is a skill to be acquired. This handbook of ethical practice is a skill-building resource that will help victim assistance providers think through common ethical dilemmas. It offers practical tools and problem-solving techniques for addressing ethical challenges as they develop. Readers have the chance to assess their personal values, moral orientation, and personal bias to consider how these elements influence the decisions they make in the workplace. Exercises in ethical decision-making allow individuals and groups the benefit of forethought: the chance to practice the process through which common dilemmas are solved in a workshop environment.

Support and services to crime victims takes many different forms and, as a result, not all victim assistance providers are subject to the same ethical standards. This text strives to be inclusive in its analysis of elements that influence ethical responsibility. Oftentimes, how a victim assistance provider responds to an ethical challenge is dependent on the nature of the service he or she provides. Consider the following scenario.

Jo Kumar is an eighteen-year-old college freshman and the victim of a drugged-induced sexual assault at a fraternity party. A medical examiner has confirmed physical injuries consistent with sexual assault and the presence of rohypnol in her bloodstream. Three seniors will be charged. During the investigation, Jo has formed a close relationship with victim assistance provider Natasha Sphinx. On the afternoon before the hearing, Natasha receives a frantic call from Jo, who says, "I can't go through with this." She tells Natasha that on one occasion the previous summer she had taken a "roofie" (slang for rohypnol) for fun at a party. Jo is afraid that she will be asked on the witness stand if she has ever taken the drug voluntarily. "If I admit to taking rohypnol no one will believe I was raped."

There are few instances where differences in priorities among victim assistance providers are more apparent than in cases of sexual assault that involve questions of confidentiality. On one hand, confidentiality is sacrosanct to a rape crisis counselor. In that role, Natasha would keep Jo's revelation in confidence. Together they would discuss the situation and review the possible options and outcomes. Natasha would then let Jo make her own decision as to how to handle the information.

If Natasha is a system-based service provider, however, Jo's right to confidentiality would be superceded by Natasha's obligation to pass on important information about the case to her colleagues. While prior consumption of an illegal drug should not be a factor in Jo's case, "date rape" laws call for increased penalties for drug-induced sexual assaults. Therefore, the possibility of *voluntary* consumption becomes an issue in the case.

Additional factors may come into play. Jo's father is a Hindu immigrant who condemns any kind of sexual activity before marriage. If he learns about the victimization, he will blame Jo and punish her severely. Whether she works in a community-based or system-based environment, Natasha's sensitivity to cultural values becomes an important element in her handling of the case. Other issues—victim-blaming, right to self-determination, and standards of professional conduct—may impact the situation, as well as practical considerations that will affect how Jo and Natasha attempt to resolve the problem.

Victim assistance providers spend their workdays negotiating complex issues that arise following a criminal victimization and striving for the best outcomes possible. It is a good and moral endeavor. Hence, one might ask, "What does ethics have to do with the work of serving crime victims?" when questions over ethical action imply positive or negative moral judgments. Before embarking on a study of ethics in victim services, it is important to clarify the difference between acting ethically and adhering to a code of professional ethics.

Ethics are systems of moral values. *Professional ethics* are sets of standards, based on proven and sound principles of conduct and quality of service, created from within a profession as a means of articulating what constitutes excellence in the field. Professional ethical standards are most effective when they are generated from within associations based on the knowledge and the skills of the members.

Victim assistance providers who are familiar with the ethical standards of the profession will know that confidentiality, recognizing the interests of the person served as the primary responsibility, professional competence, and understanding legal responsibilities are all ethical standards that will impact Natasha's decision-making process. Her level of cultural competency is relevant because Jo's father's values may lead him to blame Jo for the victimization and inhibit her capacity to heal. In addition, the nature of Natasha's employment, whether community-based or system-based, predetermines some of the ethical decisions that she will make assisting Jo.

Since the late 1960s, the field of victim assistance has evolved from a grassroots movement of committed individuals and nonprofit organizations into a professional discipline. It now encompasses a wide diversity of organized community- and system-based individuals and organizations whose service to crime victims range the entire gamut of the criminal justice experience. While there is no consensus on every aspect of the ethics of victim services, "putting victims first" remains the mantra of the field.

As this evolution has continued, victim assistance providers on many fronts have called for a definition of *professionalism*. Common questions include:

What constitutes excellence in the delivery of services to crime victims?

What does it mean to be well trained and well informed?

How do we formalize accountability?

How do we build credibility in the broader criminal justice arena?

These inquiries are only natural for a movement increasingly recognized by the juvenile and criminal justice systems, academia, and the public at large as a credible, worthwhile, and much-needed service.

In an effort to address common goals around excellence in the delivery of services to crime victims, in 1999 the Office for Victims of Crime created the National Victim Assistance Standards Consortium (NVASC). NVASC's goal was to create a model for competency and ethical standards of conduct for the field of victim assistance. To do this, the Consortium researched existing standards in similar professions, polled the field of victim assistance, and utilized the expertise and experience of a representative and diverse core of victim assistance professionals. The result of this work is the *NVASC Standards for Victim Assistance Programs and Providers*, written by Dana DeHart, Ph.D., at the University of South Carolina at Columbia.

This book, *Ethics in Victim Services,* is based on the NVASC model of ethical standards. It is designed to help victim assistance professionals identify, analyze, and resolve the many ethical dilemmas they face on a daily basis. It provides victim service providers with the tools to develop model ethical standards appropriate for their organizations and agencies. Neither the NVASC standards, nor this book, are intended to dictate standards of performance.

The text is divided into two parts. Part 1, "Recognizing and Resolving Ethical Conflict," discusses the following topics:

Chapter 1, "Ethical Standards of the NVASC," traces the history of ethics and professional ethics as they have developed from the classical theorists who contemplated good and evil to the associations that wrote modern codes of professional ethics for doctors and social workers to the late-twentieth-century philosophers who tackled prejudice, feminism, and oppression. The chapter examines the professional values upon which the NVASC ethical code is based and discusses each NVASC ethical standard in detail.

"Ethics and Self-Awareness" (chapter 2) offers resources for analyzing personal values and understanding moral and cultural orientations that influence relationships with crime victims. It looks at cultural competency as a prerequisite for effective ethical decision-making, and it discusses how the difference in roles and responsibilities of community- and system-based victim assistance providers impacts the ethical decision-making process.

The third chapter, "Ethical Issues and Legal Concerns," focuses in depth on the more complex and challenging of the ethical standards, that is, boundaries, confidentiality and exceptions to confidentiality, and legal responsibilities.

Chapter 4, "Managing Ethical Dilemmas," discusses ineffective problem-solving techniques that lead to ethical dilemmas, problem-solving techniques to avoid ethical dilemmas, and ethical communication. The chapter presents an ethical decision-making model and guides the reader through a step-by-step process of analyzing a dilemma, looking at practical and ethical considerations, proposing various responses to the dilemma, and projecting the likely positive and negative outcomes of each response suggested.

Part 2 is a "Toolbox" for exploring the ethical decision-making process as it applies to the everyday dilemmas that occur in the delivery of services to crime victims. Nineteen case scenarios offer insights into the intention and application of the NVASC ethical standards, following the NVASC organizational format:

Scope of services

Coordinating with the community

Direct services

Administration and evaluation

When using this text, it is important to keep three points in mind:

1. *The code of ethical standards in* Ethics in Victim Services *is intended to serve as a model.* The NVASC ethical standards are representative of input from the entire field of victim assistance and are well grounded in established model codes from other professions. However, the applicability of the standards fluctuates according to the type of services provided to victims. Therefore, they should be used as a model to be adapted to the organization and agency needs.

2. *This book is designed for use by both community- and system-based victim assistance providers.* Sensitivity to the diverse needs and backgrounds of all victim assistance providers was a priority in the development of this text. These ethical standards may be implemented in any number of diverse and innovative ways that are responsive to the individualized needs of any given sector of victim assistance. The key is in acknowledging the need for ethical standards and the benefits that an established and recognized system of standards will have for victims, providers, the justice system, and the community at large.

3. *The study of ethics does not lead to easy or exact answers.* Reading this text cannot ensure that providers will always behave in professionally "ethical" ways. The practice of victim assistance inherently includes a multiplicity of complicated, and sometimes conflicting, interests, and ethical dilemmas that, by definition, do not lend themselves to clear-cut or right answers. Instead, this text is designed to assist providers in identifying and analyzing these ethical dilemmas, applying the applicable standards to the situation at hand, and arriving at a resolution. Engaging in this process is the keystone of consistent ethical professionalism.

The essence of this text is the methodology for achieving ethically responsible services to crime victims. Before it moves into the practical application of ethics, however, it looks briefly at the historical evolution of ethical theories and discusses professional ethics in modern times. Pursuit of justice and compassionate action are ethical concepts that have their roots in antiquity. How and why they evolved into standards of professional conduct in the field of victim assistance is the subject of the first chapter.

Part 1

Recognizing and Resolving Ethical Conflict

CHAPTER 1

Ethical Standards of the NVASC

Professional ethical standards for victim assistance providers creates a win-win situation for victim service providers, community organizations, the criminal and juvenile justice systems, and society as a whole. First and foremost, however, a code of ethics for victim assistance serves the best interests of victims and provides consistent, high-quality services and support. Ethical standards can ensure crime victims:

- Consistent ethical conduct on the part of all victim assistance providers
- Improved care and services
- Increased satisfaction
- Protection from potential abuses that can occur in any helping profession
- Access to better trained providers and greater uniformity in the quality of services

Developing a code of ethics in a field as diverse as victim assistance is a challenge. No single set of rules applies to every agency and organization. Conservatively, the field of victim services includes the professionals who work in community-based organizations such as rape crisis and domestic violence centers and homicide survivor groups; the providers who hold positions along the continuum of the criminal justice system, from police-based victim assistance professionals all the way to probation and parole-based providers; and allied professionals from the fields of law, medicine, social work, psychology, and education. Providers are subject to a wide variety of policy and legal authorities governing their conduct that result in different ethical priorities. These differences should be communicated between collaborating organizations to ensure delivery of quality and ethically responsible services to crime victims.

Agencies and organizations that take on the task of developing a code of professional ethics will want to define standards of excellence, create protocols through which ethical dilemmas can be resolved, and establish procedures so that conflicts and nonadherence to the code of ethics can be addressed. When providers conflict over differences in ethical priorities among victim service agencies and organizations that are required to collaborate, cross-training on professional ethics is helpful.

In addition to improving services to crime victims, the establishment of a consistent code of ethical conduct for all victim assistance providers would impact the profession in significant ways. An established code of ethics would bring:

- Increased respect for the profession
- Potential increase in the types of jobs, as well as the level of remuneration
- Greater opportunities for advancement in the field
- Heightened personal satisfaction in working in a clearly defined and established helping profession

Because the trend in criminal justice has been to focus on the offender and the offender's rights, expanding the public mindset to include victims has been a difficult task. Some of the mass victimizations and acts of terrorism that have occurred over the last several years have done much to publicize the plight of crime victims in this country. But the establishment of a professional code of ethics will go a long way toward publicly validating the field of victim assistance and bringing greater attention to the need for effective assistance for crime victims. With the adoption of a code of ethics, society at large will recognize victim assistance not only as a profession, but as a profession offering a valuable service by successfully helping victims to return as fully as possible to whatever role in society they may occupy.

Before looking at the professional values in the victim assistance profession and the NVASC code of professional ethics, it is useful to consider how society has come to think about morals, values, and ethical conduct and why professionals formed national associations and developed codes of ethical responsibility. The next section is a brief review of the history of ethics and the development of professional ethics as a means of establishing standards of services in various professions.

History of Ethics

Since the classical Greek era, philosophers have discussed the ethics that guide human beings toward virtuous behavior. Ethics as the systematic study of moral principles can be traced back to such philosophers as Aristotle in Greece in 300 B.C., Augustine in Roman Africa in A.D. 300, and Thomas Aquinas in Italy in 1200.

In the eighteenth and nineteenth centuries, ethical models emerged as theories to promote societal well-being. For example, the most famous proponent of *utilitarianism* was John Stuart Mill (1806–73), who emphasized happiness as a baseline value in judging action. Mill writes, "Actions are right in proportion as they tend to promote happiness; wrong as they tend to produce the reverse of happiness." *Formalist ethics*, defined by Immanuel Kant (1724–1804), focuses on duty and moral obligation. He emphasizes the value of human life, writing, "Act in such a way that you treat humanity, whether in your own person or in the person of another, always at the same time as an end, and never simply as a means."

Ethical theorists during the twentieth century began to focus on injustice and inequality. A modern revision of *formalism* that has its roots in Kantian ethics is John Rawls's theory of justice. Rawls's goal is for society and institutions to arrive at a model that eliminates injustice and prejudice. He sets forth three principles:

> Everyone should have an *equal right* to the most extensive form of basic liberties.
>
> Offices and positions should be open to all under conditions of *equal opportunity*.
>
> Social and economic institutions are to be *maximally arranged to benefit those with the greatest need*.

By the late twentieth century, ethical theorists asserted values that approach the principles of advocacy, service, and support on which crime victim assistance is based. For example, the concept of *ethics of care* evolved as part of the feminist movement and focuses on establishing a caring relationship in balance with concerns about justice as fundamental aspects of ethical behavior. Ethics of care emphasizes interactions and relationships over conceptual models built on principles. Nel Noddings, Carol Gilligan, Annette Baier, and Rita Manning have all contributed to the evolution of this model. Manning, in particular, promotes two principles:

> A disposition to care is a willingness to receive others and to give attention to others' needs. A person has a *general ethical obligation to care.*

> The obligation to care for (caring as expressed by action) entails *responding to the needs of others in a caring way.* (Manning expands the obligation to include caring for the needs of communities.)

It is important to note that these writers are not proposing that ethics derived from concepts of injustice and inequality be abandoned. Baier recommends that we "make room for an ethic of love and trust, including an account of human bonding and friendship." Ethics of care validates the role of the emotions in sensing "need" and grasping the meaning of situations that may not otherwise be understood from a purely rational perspective.

Moral theorists like Paulo Freire add a new dimension to ethical theory in their discussions of the political and social paradigms that disenfranchise the poor. Freire writes about the disconnect between impoverished youth and their educational experience that perpetuates their oppression. Freire's ethical education model seeks to develop a consciousness in students that questions the nature of their historical and social circumstances. The classroom environment designed to develop this consciousness is based on three features:

> Open dialogue between students and teachers that encourages inquiry, reflection and participation

> A formation of a "community " in the classroom that has common goals and is all-inclusive

> Use of language and terminology that is relevant to the lives of the students.

Freire's goal is to teach students to critically examine the social organization of the culture they live in, and, rather than unknowingly join a disenfranchised group within that culture, to work toward balance in the power structure.

The ethical principles on which crime victim assistance is based have roots in all the models discussed in this section. Indeed, the ideals of do no harm, care for others, eliminate injustice, and treat others as one wishes to be treated inform most ethical codes in the helping professions. Precisely how these ideals are transformed into professional codes of ethics depends on the core values of the discipline and the requirements of the workplace.

History of Professional Ethics

Professional ethics developed alongside personal ethics as individuals skilled in specific disciplines organized themselves into groups. The earliest known professional code was developed in ancient Greece in the fourth century B.C. when Hippocrates initiated a movement calling for all physicians to exhibit a high level of professional and ethical behavior. As a guide for this behavior, the Hippocratic Oath was adopted by medical doctors throughout the ancient and medieval world and continues to serve as the inspiration for modern codes of ethics for the field of medicine.

Medicine was also the first profession in the modern world for which a code of ethics was written. In 1803 Dr. Thomas Percival wrote a code of professional ethics for doctors in England. Percival's code served as the model for the American Medical Association's (AMA) Code of Ethics, which was completed in 1847. Some historians report that, in adopting a code of ethics, the medical profession sought to improve its credibility following decades of unbridled abuse of the title of "doctor" by charlatans and con artists in the pioneer states. Pharmacists and lawyers were quick to follow suit with their own standards of professional ethical behavior.

Interestingly enough, until the early twentieth century, social workers and members of the other helping professions refrained from developing ethical codes. They believed that their work of helping others for little financial gain relieved them of the need to formalize their ethical standards. In 1922, however, the *Annals of the American Society for Political and Social Sciences* devoted its May 1922 issue to a discussion of ethical codes in business and professions. Following the release of the journal, many state and local chapters began drafting codes of ethics. It was not until the 1950s, however, when these state and local chapters merged into the National Association of Social Workers (NASW), that they drafted a national code of ethics, which was adopted in 1960. Since that time, the NASW Code of Ethics has been revised several times, most recently in 1999, when additions were made to the text to address specific needs and concerns of individuals.

Since the late 1990s, national and state victim assistance organizations and coalitions have drafted codes of ethics for use by their memberships. In some cases, the effort to articulate professional ethics grew out of a need to designate specific counseling protocols for victim assistance providers. Other initiatives established performance standards and paved the way for professional credentialing. In 1999 the National Victim Assistance Standards Consortium (NVASC) was formed to create standards of competency in the victim assistance profession that could be adapted as a model nationwide. The *Ethical Standards for Victim Assistance Providers* is the result of the Consortium's efforts.

Defining Values in Victim Assistance

The standards of ethics in the victim services discipline created by NVASC include a set of guiding values to support practitioners in everyday workplace decision-making. These values represent an interpretation of tried and true principles adapted from other helping professions. They include the ideals of competence, integrity, professional responsibility, respect for people's rights and dignity, concern for others' welfare, and social responsibility.

Competence

Providers should know their capabilities and exercise them at the highest possible level while being aware of the limits of their expertise. Competent providers make appropriate use of other professional resources in the community and recognize the need to seek out opportunities for ongoing professional development. Their guiding principle should be "do no harm." In addition, their ability to serve victims effectively depends on their own personal wellness, and they should place a high priority on self-care. They should also lend their support to the well-being of colleagues and agency staff.

Integrity

Honesty, fairness, and respect are fundamental qualities for victim assistance providers. They must be honest about their qualifications, be clear about their role as counselor or advocate to a victim, avoid dual relationships, and be fair in the fulfillment of their commitments. They must seek to understand how their personal history and belief systems may affect their interactions with others.

Professional Responsibility

Professionally responsible victim assistance providers always maintain professional standards of conduct—both inside and outside the agency. When they are concerned about the conduct of their colleagues, they communicate with them to help prevent unethical behavior. When they collaborate with other professionals or institutions, they serve the best interests of the victim. They keep their personal values personal and do not compromise professional responsibilities or behave in a manner that might reduce public trust in victim services.

Respect for People's Rights and Dignity

Victim assistance providers must respect the fundamental rights, dignity, and worth of all people and be committed to the victim's right to privacy, confidentiality, and self-determination. They must value justice and equality, be aware of their personal biases, and not discriminate in the delivery or quality of service.

Concern for Others' Welfare

Providers who are actively concerned with the welfare of those they serve and those with whom they collaborate must act compassionately and with sensitivity to the real and ascribed differences in power between themselves and others. They must not abuse their position or exploit or mislead people during or after the professional relationship. When conflicts occur, providers must attempt to fulfill their duties in a manner that causes the least amount of harm to all involved.

Social Responsibility

Providers must educate themselves about their professional, legal, and social responsibilities and be committed to the reduction of crime and victimization. They must work toward the development of laws and policies that support the interests of victims and be committed to social justice and to the well-being of everyone.

This set of guiding values represent the foundation from which the NVASC has developed the following nineteen standards of professional conduct to guide victim assistance providers in their resolution of common ethical challenges.

NVASC Ethical Standards

Section 1: Scope of Services

Ethical Standard 1.1: The victim assistance provider understands his or her legal responsibilities, limitations, and the implications of his/her actions within the service delivery setting and performs duties in accord with laws, regulations, policies, and legislated rights of persons served.

Clearly, the scope of this ethical standard is broad, and includes the statutory and constitutional rights of the victim at both the state and federal level. It also includes any regulations or policies that may be in place in the particular state where the crime occurred. Service providers *must* know all the statutes that govern all aspects of victims' rights and services in their state and they must act within the scope of those statutes. And while knowing these statutes may seem relatively straightforward, applying them can be complicated. Many agencies do not provide this type of training at an entry level. Others do not provide it at all but expect service providers to gain this knowledge on their own or on the job. A victim assistance provider who has an insufficient knowledge of the specifics of the legal authority under which he or she works may unintentionally follow unethical practices, violate the law, and/or cause harm to the victim.

Service providers must know whether or not they can be subpoenaed in court to testify about information shared with them by their clients. In some states, confidential communications between community-based sexual assault and domestic violence advocates and their clients are protected by law. Currently, this privilege does not extend to system-based victim advocates.

Ethical Standard 1.2: *The victim assistance provider accurately represents his or her professional title, qualifications, and/or credentials in relationships with persons served and in public advertising.*

The professional and educational credentials of all victim assistance providers that pertain to their positions should be disclosed in order to avoid any misconceptions or misunderstandings about their role in the context of service to the victim or their responsibilities to the agency and their colleagues.

Victim assistance providers should exercise discretion in terms of self-promotion or advertisement. For example, they should not represent themselves as counselors, therapists, or specialists in a specific type of advocacy if they have not received the training and accreditation that the discipline requires. They are discouraged from using victim testimonials or descriptions of the uniqueness of their services as a means of self-promotion.

Ethical Standard 1.3: *The victim assistance provider maintains a high standard of professional conduct.*

Like other professionals, victim assistance providers must aspire to a high degree of professionalism. This means that providers must not only avoid improper behavior, but avoid even the *appearance* of impropriety. In maintaining a high degree of professional conduct, providers must not use their positions to obtain special favors, privileges, advantages, gifts, or access to services that are unrelated to agency interests or that serve them personally. Moreover, providers must distinguish between agency and personal points of view, and refrain from communicating a personal viewpoint as if it were agency opinion or policy.

Ethical Standard 1.4: *The victim assistance provider achieves and maintains a high level of professional competence.*

Victim assistance providers must keep informed of all new and pertinent developments within the field, including research findings, newly enacted statutory guidelines, and policy changes. Achieving and maintaining professional competence serve the interests of the victim, the field of victim services, and the victim assistance provider.

Being competent also means providers must recognize when the need for supervision or other types of consultation arises. In serving the best needs of the victim, providers must stay within the clearly defined range of their roles and responsibilities. If the victims' needs go beyond these particular skills, providers must make an outside referral. To do this, providers must be familiar with the resources of the communities in which they work and have contacts with the allied professionals in the area.

In maintaining professional competence, providers must also be aware of the signs of severe stress and burnout and develop adequate resources for caring for themselves, such as talking with colleagues, participating in support groups, and maintaining a proper diet and exercise regime. Clearly, it is critical that providers refrain from providing services if impaired by medication, alcohol, drugs, or any other substance, or when suffering from a physical or mental impairment that interferes with the performance of their duties.

Ethical Standard 1.5: *The victim assistance provider who provides a service for a fee informs a person served about the fee at the initial session or meeting.*

The discussion of any and all financial arrangements must take place at the outset of the relationship between a provider and the victim. Full and accurate information concerning when payment is expected, whether insurance may cover any expenses, how payment is handled, and the policy regarding missed or canceled appointments must be clearly communicated before services are delivered.

Bartering, that is, the trading of goods or services for victim assistance services, is not appropriate except in situations wherein the victim's culture provides for such customs and it would be offensive to the victim to refuse such an arrangement. However, these arrangements can only be made with the full knowledge of the provider's supervisor. The key is to ensure that the bartering arrangement will not create a potential conflict of interest.

Section 2: Coordinating within the Community

Ethical Standard 2.1: *The victim assistance provider conducts relationships with colleagues and other professionals in such a way as to promote mutual respect, public confidence, and improvement of service.*

Since the field of victim services is one of public service, it is important for providers to contribute, whenever and wherever possible, to public confidence and respect for their agency and the field. Furthermore, the ethical standard regarding professional conduct requires that when making statements in a public context, providers should clarify if they are speaking on their own behalf, as a representative of their agency, or on behalf of all victim assistance providers.

Ethical Standard 2.2: *The victim assistance provider shares knowledge and encourages proficiency in victim assistance among colleagues and other professionals.*

Victim assistance providers must be ready, willing, and eager to share their knowledge, expertise, and skills with other practitioners both in and out of the workplace, including both paid and volunteer workers. In the case of volunteer workers, victim assistance providers should do everything within their power to ensure that volunteers have access to the information, training, and resources they need to do their jobs properly and effectively.

Knowledge sharing in the field of victim assistance should be carried out with an overall view to the continuing improvement of the quality of victim services. Particularly in the field of victim assistance, service to victims involves a team approach and the willingness to share with and listen to colleagues from various cultures, disciplines, philosophies, and allied professions.

Ethical Standard 2.3: *The victim assistance provider serves the public interest by contributing to the improvement of systems that impact victims of crime.*

With respect to the attainment of their own program goals, providers are expected to take part in professional or community activities that actively encourage or support these goals. They are also encouraged to support and/or take part in other activities, professional, community, or otherwise, that generally support the goals of victim services, including the improvement of justice system(s), victim services, and/or access to such services.

Section 3: Direct Services

Ethical Standard 3.1: *The victim assistance provider respects and attempts to protect the victim's civil rights.*

In addition to basic civil rights, many state statutes and guidelines provide for the protection of other rights, including the following:

1. The victim retains all basic civil rights in the professional relationship.

2. The victim retains the right not to be discriminated against in the

provision of services on the basis of race/ethnicity, language, sex/gender, age, sexual orientation, (dis)ability, social class, economic status, education, marital status, religious affiliation, residency, or HIV status.

3. The victim retains the right to release her or his confidential information and records and have that right protected.

4. The victim retains the right to know any and all exceptions to the confidentiality privilege, including the victim assistance provider's mandates to report child abuse and elder abuse as applicable by state and federal law. The exceptions to the confidentiality privilege vary from state to state and will be discussed in greater detail later in this chapter (Ethical Standard 3.5). All victim assistance providers must be thoroughly informed about the applicable statutory authority regarding confidentiality and other basic civil rights within their state and/or jurisdiction.

Ethical Standard 3.2: The victim assistance provider recognizes the interests of the person served as a primary responsibility.

A victim's desires and wants with respect to the situation may contradict options offered by the victim assistance provider. The provider should advocate for what the victim desires (see Ethical Standard 3.4) and for what is in his or her best interests within the limits of ethical standards, program policy, and state and federal laws. It is never appropriate for a provider to offer a service only if a victim agrees to a particular course of action. A provider may deeply disagree with a victim's proposed course of action, or nonaction, but the only ethical response is to provide as much information as possible so that the victim can make a fully informed choice. If a conflict develops between the provider and the victim over these choices, the provider should explain the situation, make a referral for an alternative provider, and/or seek outside assistance to resolve the issue.

Ethical Standard 3.3: The victim assistance provider refrains from behaviors that communicate victim blame, suspicion regarding victim accounts of the crime, condemnation for past behavior, or other judgmental, antivictim sentiment.

To maintain professional trust with the victim and effectively advocate on his or her behalf, a victim assistance provider must be vigilant to avoid doing or saying anything that might communicate suspicion, blame, doubt, or condemnation of the victim's actions, nonactions, feelings, beliefs, and so on, about the crime.

Ethical Standard 3.4: *The victim assistance provider respects the victim's right to self-determination.*

Victims have the most informed perspective regarding their personal history, victimization, and risk, and therefore they have ultimate authority over their interests. If the provider's perceptions of what is best for a victim are at odds with that victim's point of view, information can be presented to enhance the victim's perspective. Ultimately, the provider should encourage victims to make their own decisions. As discussed above, the services offered by providers are determined by the applicable state and federal laws, regulations, and agency policies. If there is a conflict between what the victim wants and the applicable state, federal, or agency authority, then the provider must take steps to resolve that conflict, including:

> Verbal disclosure of the conflict to the victim;
>
> Consultation with a colleague or supervisor; and
>
> Possible referral to an outside professional for further services and/or resolution of the conflict.

Ethical Standard 3.5: *The victim assistance provider preserves the confidentiality of information provided by the person served or acquired from other sources before, during, and after the course of the professional relationship.*

Ethically speaking, the Consortium Standard 3.5 requires the preservation of confidentiality at all times other than the exceptions listed below. These exceptions are generally accepted in the field of victim services and other helping professions. A violation of confidentiality can be extremely harmful to the victim; it can also potentially leave the victim assistance provider and/or his or her agency open to legal liability. Therefore, all providers should make it their mission to understand confidentiality and all of its nuances.

Information about confidentiality should be provided to the victim at the first meeting, or at least at the first available opportunity if exigencies of the first meeting do not allow it. Furthermore, providers must be aware of all legal authority governing confidentiality in their jurisdiction, as well as agency policies that may apply. Sample state laws regarding confidential privilege are discussed in chapter 3. Since confidentiality is a complex area of ethical consideration, due care should be taken by all providers to be fully informed and continually current regarding any and all legal, statutory, policy, and agency authority.

Exceptions to the Consortium's Ethical Standard 3.5 include:

- In the course of formally reporting, conferring, or consulting with administrative superiors, colleagues, or consultants who share professional responsibility, in which instance all recipients of such information are similarly bound to regard the communication as confidential.
- With the written consent of the person who provided the information.
- In case of death or disability, with the written consent of a personal representative, or the beneficiary of an insurance policy on the person's life, health, or physical condition. (Special consideration may be given to domestic violence cases or other cases in which disability may have been inflicted by the personal representative, for example, if a batterer is the personal representative, disclosure of confidential communications could put the victim at future risk.)
- When a communication reveals the intended commission of a crime or harmful act and such disclosure is judged necessary to protect any person from a clear, imminent risk of serious mental or physical harm or injury, or to thwart a serious threat to the public safety.
- When a medical emergency occurs and the victim is not able to authorize the release of information, information limited to the medical emergency may be disclosed.
- The mandated reporting of abuse of a child or a vulnerable adult.
- When the person waives the confidentiality by bringing any public charges against the provider.

Additionally, the service of minor victims may require exceptions to confidentiality; this is also governed by individual state laws. Victim assistance providers are encouraged to communicate confidentiality to minors in terms that they can understand, and to preserve such confidentiality unless compelling reasons require the notification of parents or guardians.

In disclosing information regarding confidentiality or in communicating to a victim the fact that certain confidential information may need to be disclosed, the provider should be prepared to address the victim's reaction to this disclosure. While a provider or agency cannot provide specific confidential information for statistical purposes, it is appropriate to provide it without identifying its source.

Ethical Standard 3.6: *The victim assistance provider avoids conflicts of interest and discloses any possible conflict to the program or person served, as well as to prospective programs or persons served.*

Victim assistance providers should not engage in efforts that involve conflicting influences or loyalties that compromise the best interest of the persons or agency served, whether these conflicts are based on professional, personal, family, business, or other relationships. Conflicts of interest can arise as the result of past professional relationships, either within the current position or through some past employment.

Previous relationships, be they familial, professional, personal, or business, with individuals who come to a victim assistance provider for services create potential conflicts of interest. Providers who have survived a crime and, as a result, have entered the field of victim services may at times be tempted to refer to their own victimization during the counseling relationship with another victim. The transfer of focus from the client victim's experience to the provider's experience can be considered another kind of conflict of interest. Victim assistance providers must be rigorous in their efforts to discern potential conflicts of interest and step down from any job where the conflict will lessen the quality of service they deliver.

Ethical Standard 3.7: *The victim assistance provider terminates a professional relationship with a victim when the victim is not likely to benefit from continued services.*

When a victim no longer benefits from the services the victim assistance provider has to offer or the services are no longer relevant to his or her needs, the professional relationship should be terminated. The provider should prepare the victim for this eventuality, particularly if the victim is unusually vulnerable and/or derives a great deal of support from their relationship. If referral to another professional is indicated, the provider should obtain as much information as possible and provide this to the victim in a timely manner. On the other hand, providers are strongly discouraged from terminating a relationship with a victim in order to pursue a business or personal relationship with the victim.

Ethical Standard 3.8: *The victim assistance provider does not engage in personal relationships with persons served which exploit professional trust or which could impair the victim assistance provider's objectivity and professional judgment.*

Dual relationships are sometimes difficult to avoid, particularly in small communities; for example, a victim assistance provider may be asked to serve a neighbor or the child of a friend. The application of the standard to avoid dual relationships is therefore explored in the context of the potential to cause harm. Whenever there is the potential for loss of objectivity, conflict of interest, or the exploitation of a victim seeking help, the mixing of personal and professional roles is not appropriate.

When a provider cannot avoid a personal or business relationship with a client, the provider should seek counsel and supervision from colleagues regarding his or her objectivity regarding the case. If a personal or business relationship with an individual has existed prior to the professional relationship, the provider should determine whether or not his or her judgment may be impaired in the delivery of services in the best interests of the client.

Under any circumstance, sexual relationships with victims are the most serious violations of this ethical standard. Furthermore, a provider should not behave in a way that verbally or physically indicates sexual interest or sexual harassment with current or former clients. It is the provider's responsibility to act appropriately with clients with respect to dual relationships regardless of the client's attempts to initiate a personal or business relationship.

Ethical Standard 3.9: *The victim assistance provider does not discriminate against a victim or another staff member on the basis of race/ethnicity, language, sex/gender, age, sexual orientation, (dis)ability, social class, economic status, education, marital status, religious affiliation, residency, or HIV status.*

A victim assistance provider who is unable to provide services to a victim(s) because of bias or prejudice must inform his or her superiors of the potential bias. Personal bias might be explored through the use of self-inventory tools (such as the one presented in chapter 2). If there is any doubt about a provider's ability to offer judgment-free and objective assistance, the provider should seek consultation and/or supervision. In addition, the need for multicultural competency (described in detail in chapter 2), while not a Consortium standard, is an important factor in the resolution of ethical dilemmas that involve victims of ethnically and culturally diverse communities.

Ethical Standard 3.10: *The victim assistance provider furnishes opportunities for colleague victim assistance providers to seek appropriate services when traumatized by a criminal event or client interaction.*

In some cases, it may be appropriate for victim assistance providers to offer assistance and feedback to colleagues who have been traumatized by a crime or client interaction. It is common for victim assistance providers to "process" traumatic events or other difficulties experienced in the course of their everyday jobs. Because of limited resources, it may be difficult—if not impossible—for providers to pursue outside intervention or support. However, if possible, providers who are in need of formal support in the wake of trauma should try to seek assistance from allied professions or providers in other jurisdictions, so as to minimize the possibility of potential professional conflicts of interest.

Section 4: Administration and Evaluation

Ethical Standard 4.1: *The victim assistance provider reports to appropriate authorities the conduct of any colleague or other professional (including oneself) that constitutes mistreatment of a person served or that brings the profession into dishonor.*

A victim assistance provider must report clear violations of ethical standards to the appropriate authorities. This would include governing boards, funding entities, administrators, and supervisors. The victim assistance provider should never knowingly participate in actions that violate ethical standards. Furthermore, providers are encouraged to self-report violations that require a written report be filed.

Conclusion

Since the classical Greek era, ethicists have contemplated codes of human behavior that manifest their values and belief systems. As societies expanded and grew more complex, ethical theories increased in scope from rules of behavior for individuals to rules that addressed societal well-being. Professional ethics have grown out of a need to set performance standards within specific disciplines. The field of victim assistance has now matured to the point where a code of ethics has become useful to establish standards of excellence in the delivery of services to crime victims. Implementing a code of ethics, however, requires more than a cursory reading of the rules. In the next chapter, providers will be introduced to some of the key factors that may influence their ability to effectively address the ethical challenges that arise when assisting crime victims.

References

Baier, A. 1995. "What Do Women Want in a Moral Theory?" In *Moral Prejudice: Essays on Ethics*. Cambridge: Harvard University Press.

DeHart, D. D. 2003. *NVASC Standards for Victim Assistance Programs and Providers*. Columbia: University of South Carolina, Center for Child and Family Studies.

Freire, Paulo. 1993. *Pedagogy of the Oppressed*. Translated by M. Ramos. New York: Continuum.

Gilligan, C. 1982. *In a Different Voice*. Cambridge: Harvard University Press.

Kant, I. 1993. *Grounding for a Metaphysics of Morals*. Translated by J. Ellington. Indianapolis: Hackett.

Manning, R. 1992. *Speaking from the Heart*. Lanham, Md.: Rowman and Littlefield.

Mills, J. 1990. *Utilitarianism*. Edited by George Sher. Indianapolis: Hackett.

Noddings, N. 1984. *Caring: A Feminist Approach to Ethics*. Berkeley: University of California Press.

Rawls, J. 1995. *Political Liberalism*. New York: Columbia University Press.

CHAPTER 2

Ethics and Self-Awareness

Providing quality services to the victims of crime depends on many factors, but begins with the personality, moral orientation, and subjective beliefs and opinions of the victim service provider. Victim services are about relationships between providers and crime victims. Therefore, the personal values of the provider and the ethical codes that support these values will directly influence his or her interactions in the relationship. For that reason, providers need tools for assessing their personal moral orientation so that they understand what influences them in their professional domain. This chapter is designed to introduce victim assistance providers to some of those tools.

Before beginning, consider the following terms and their definitions.

Values are the ideals or beliefs that an individual or group aspire to.

Morals relate to making decisions between right and wrong.

Ethics is the articulation of standards of behavior that reflect those values or morals.

Keep in mind how these terms are used in the following text.

The Need for Self-Awareness

For more than a decade the helping professions have been grappling with issues of ethics and self-awareness. To help address this issue, Marcia Abramson, a prominent writer on ethics in the social work profession, poses a series of questions on values and ethics in an article called "Reflections on Knowing Oneself Ethically." Abramson's questions fall into seven categories that are listed here to set up a form of inquiry for victim assistance providers to analyze their personal values and increase their level of ethical self-awareness.

Prejudgments

For providers, the first step toward increasing ethical self-awareness is to understand their own worldviews. Providers should ask themselves the following two questions:

> How do I see myself in terms of race, ethnicity, class, gender, age, religion, sexual orientation, and power?

> How do my personal attitudes and experiences create stereotypes and foster biased reactions?

For example, Randy arrives at the domestic violence center heavily bruised and looking for shelter after a fight with her lesbian partner. The shelter advocate gets distracted by the question of who will share a room with Randy and unintentionally conveys to Randy that she is unwelcome. Self-awareness, prejudgments, and multicultural competency are looked at in greater detail below (see "Multicultural Competency and Ethical Challenges").

Character and Virtue

People who are self-aware steer clear of activities and actions that make them feel bad about themselves and instead seek out activities that make them feel positive and satisfied. Providers should ask themselves the following questions:

> What do I believe it means to be a good member of society?

> What actions or behaviors make me feel like I have been a good person, done my jobs well, or contributed to society at large?

> What actions or behaviors make me feel like a responsible employee of the agency or organization?

> What actions or behaviors make me feel like I have done right by the victim that I am serving?

> What do I believe are the characteristics of a competent victim assistance provider?

What do I believe are the characteristics of a good victim assistance provider in terms of professional standards and ethics?

What do I believe are the characteristics of a morally good person?

When those roles conflict, which role am I likely to choose?

For example, Sharon wants to help Kiki, a stalking victim, to move out of town with her two children but there are no funds in the center budget to pay for the relocation. Sharon's brother is a landlord with a vacant apartment in a nearby town and he owes her a favor. She is tempted to call in the favor by asking for a few months' free lodging for Kiki and helping the family move over the weekend. If Sharon did not have a professional relationship with Kiki, she would not hesitate to help her. Sharon wants to be morally good but taking the initiative to move Kiki might conflict with center policies and ethical standards.

Moral Orientations

Moral orientations affect the ethical decision-making processes. Victim assistance providers should try to understand which of a number of moral orientations might influence the way they arrive at decisions when they are presented with dilemmas. On which of the following moral orientations are their personal values founded?

Religion: Do I follow the guidance of a higher spiritual power (e.g., God, Allah, Buddha)?

Conscience: Do I refer to my own internal sounding board?

Duty: Do I believe in doing my duty within the context of my social or professional role (i.e., parent, police officer, victim assistance provider)? As a victim assistance provider, how does my duty conflict with my desire to serve?

Respect: Do I believe all people should be treated with respect? Under what conditions might a person not deserve to be treated with respect?

Human rights: Do I believe in establishing minimal moral standards of human decency (i.e., the Bill of Rights)? When the law does not support the rights of victims, how do I respond?

Utility: Do I believe that making the world a better place, reducing suffering, and increasing happiness means considering the consequences for everyone? How does the utilitarian value impact my attitude toward those who victimize?

Justice: Do I believe fairness for one means fairness for all? Serving victims and seeking justice are both critical to the victims' rights movement. Which of the two values is the greater motivator, and why?

Virtue: Do I try to be a good person and assume good people will make good decisions? How does the value of being virtuous apply in the field of victim assistance?

Truth or Consequences

Victim assistance providers should ask themselves the following question:

Do I adhere to a principle because it is the right thing to do even though doing so may result in negative consequences? For example, is it better to lie (or omit the truth) if doing so avoids potentially harmful consequences?

Spirituality

Victim assistance providers should ask themselves the following questions:

Do I understand how my spiritual beliefs affect the provider-client relationships, particularly when the victim's beliefs are different from my own? What are some of the occasions where spiritual sensitivity might be critical to serving the crime victim effectively?

Individual Rights versus the Good of the Community

Victim assistance providers should ask themselves the following questions:

Do I believe in protecting the victim's right to privacy and autonomy even when those rights conflict with the well-being of society at large? Under what conditions might I not believe in protecting the victim's right to privacy?

In dealing with a problem, am I more likely to act on my own or to seek the advice of family and friends and incorporate their views into my decision-making process? How might the outcome be different?

The Voice of Justice versus the Voice of Caring

Victim assistance providers should ask themselves the following questions:

Do I perceive dilemmas as conflicts between the rights of the individuals involved and strive to resolve them according to the principles of justice?

Do I rely on relationship building and connection, approaching moral dilemmas within their context? How does care for the client in the context of a moral dilemma affect the outcome?

Am I consistent in my approach?

Knowing oneself ethically requires self-awareness. It is important that providers understand their own definition of a morally good person. They must understand how their personal values may influence their response to challenging situations, how their religious beliefs may influence their judgments, and how their attitudes toward the rights of individuals may come into conflict with the broader principles of justice. By increasing their awareness of their personal values, they will be better prepared to face some of the challenges that will arise as they work to serve both victims and justice—the core values of their profession.

Personal Values in Action

As important as it is to understand their moral orientation, providers must also understand how willing they are to act on their values and to uphold their personal ethics if they are challenged. Being aware of the need for action, determining the right course of action, and having the emotional and intellectual commitment to follow through are all important factors when assessing personal values.

Victim assistance providers should remember that when ethical challenges arise, they may have little time to distinguish between right and wrong before they are required to react. Inaction is often the fallback position when stressful events happen too quickly to think through the appropriate response. Socrates' advice to "know thyself" is a reminder of the importance of undertaking a serious moral inventory. Few know the strength of their moral fiber or the depth of their character until it is tested. Victim assistance providers sometimes have only a minute to decide what is right or wrong.

The following scenario is an example of a stressful situation that created an ethical challenge and required a quick and ethically sensitive response. Providers should read the scenario, consider the options, and ask themselves the following questions to reflect on their ability to take action quickly in ways that manifest their personal values: Was the response highly effective? Adequate? Ineffective? Disappointing? Could proactive measures have been taken to allow for better responses under pressure in the future?

> Sam is a community-based crisis responder who is called out on a homicide in Little Saigon, a city neighborhood where many of the Asian immigrants reside. Sam speaks Vietnamese. Neighbors have witnessed the shooting of a teenage boy and the alleged killer has been arrested. The emergency medical team is preparing to remove the body to the morgue when the boy's parents arrive. They insist that the body cannot be moved until the monk arrives to pray for their son. The police officer in charge proceeds with the removal while a crowd, shouting Vietnamese, grows at the crime scene. The situation escalates. Sam introduces himself to the survivor family and learns that a Buddhist monk is on the way who will conduct a short ceremony to support the boy's departing soul.

What are some of Sam's options?

a. Sam tells the parents he is very sorry for their loss and leaves them a referral card. An elderly man in ochre robes with a shaved head runs up the sidewalk as the boy's body is driven away. The parents are devastated.

b. If he has the opportunity to speak to the officer in charge, Sam asks on behalf of the parents if they can wait for the monk to say a prayer before the body is moved. A moment later, the monk arrives, lights a candle, silences the crowd, and for a few moments he prays over the young man's body.

c. If Sam has no access to the police officer and the boy's body is removed, Sam speaks to the Buddhist monk afterwards and learns that it is a religious belief that disturbing the body at the time of death interferes with rebirth. When Sam returns to his office, he suggests to his supervisor that the team conduct outreach in the immigrant communities and develop crisis response that is spiritually sensitive.

As a crisis responder, Sam is trained to deal with stressful situations where skill at evaluating emergencies and making immediate and appropriate decisions is critical. The more passive response, option *a*, does nothing to satisfy the family's need to see their son blessed before he is taken away. Furthermore, Sam's lack of familiarity with Vietnamese Buddhist custom leaves him unprepared for the crowd reaction, which further traumatizes the boy's family. In option *b*, Sam might have convinced the officer in charge to permit a prayer ceremony, but the interaction with an officer at a homicide could be outside the scope of his response protocol. At the same time, permission to interact with a body at a crime scene is rarely granted because it becomes evidence in the investigation. Option *c* does little to satisfy the immediate need of the family but paves the way for a more sensitive response to the needs of the Buddhist community over the long term.

Sam's dilemma takes on greater significance when it is placed in the context of multicultural competency as an ethical standard, which is discussed later in this chapter.

Personal and Professional Values

Professional values grow from the same basic desire as personal values, to do no harm, help others, and make the world a better place, but they are different in focus and content. The victim assistance provider's personal values will influence his or her appreciation of the professional values of victim assistance; however, these values are not interchangeable.

A conflict between providers' personal and professional values could affect their ethical decision-making process and compromise their capacity to serve effectively in a particular circumstance. Therefore, personal values must be recognized and dealt with appropriately. Searching for ethical self-knowledge is necessary if they are to understand their innate reactions when value conflicts appear.

When providing services to victims of crime, it is providers' professional values (as described in chapter 1) that must be the key determinants in the ethical decision-making process. Their competency, integrity, responsibility, respect for the victim's right to self-determination, concern for others' welfare, and social responsibility are the professional values they will rely on to help them deliver ethically responsible services. If a situation requires them to choose one objective over another, it is these values that will inform their choices.

Competing Priorities: Personal and Professional Ethics

Some of the ethical questions that victim assistance providers may face in the service of crime victims will revolve around personal issues. Competing priorities are part of modern life and it is not unusual that the pursuit of personal interests has the potential to conflict with professional responsibilities. That is why it is important that providers develop the tools they need to recognize and resolve situations where their personal interests might cause ethical conflicts in their work. This can be done by identifying their personal ethical standards, coming to terms with the values they support, and becoming aware of their significance in the ongoing service to crime victims.

For example, when providers have personal interests in their relationships with clients, colleagues, or outside agencies and organizations, the objective exercise of their duties and responsibilities may be affected. Not only will providers' personal perceptions be challenged, but there may be viable reasons for acting in ways that could be contrary to a victim's interests.

Conflicts of Interest

Competing priorities between personal interests and professional responsibilities become conflicts of interest when the following dynamics are present:

> A personal or private interest.

> A personal or private interest that conflicts with the provider's official duty.

> A personal or private interest that interferes with the provider's objective professional judgment and is therefore a legitimate concern for those relying on the provider to be professional.

Some examples of personal activities that create professional conflicts of interest in the field of victim assistance include dual relationships, inappropriate use of confidential information, and accepting unofficial perks. (For a detailed description of the NVASC Ethical Standard 3.6 on the avoidance of professional conflicts of interest, see chapters 1 and 5.)

Whenever possible, it is best to avoid any situation where there is even a potential conflict of interest. Conflicts of interest can limit the providers' ability to act in the best interest of the persons served and/or interfere with their independent judgment. Trust is the core issue. Conflicts of interest involve the abuse, either actual or potential, of the trust people have placed in providers as professionals.

Much of the skill providers need to resolve the small day-to-day ethical questions that arise will come from on-the-job experience or from the advice and support of colleagues. When a provider is faced with unavoidable ethical concerns, open communication with colleagues on these matters will be invaluable. It is important that providers share their concerns with trusted colleagues and test their professional objectivity in questionable situations.

Multicultural Competency

Sometimes, providers' own cultural biases and/or limited understanding of other ethnicities and cultures can result in ethical conflicts that have important and far-reaching consequences for the delivery of services to crime victims. This area of potential ethical conflict should be taken into account as providers assess their personal values and moral orientation relative to their work. Raising provider awareness of these ethical challenges is the first step toward addressing them.

In 1995 the American Counseling Association (ACA) revised its ethical standards to require that counselors not discriminate based on race, ethnicity, culture, class, religion, spirituality, disability, marital status, gender, age, and/or sexual orientation in the delivery of services. These revised standards state that counselors should "actively attempt to understand the diverse cultural backgrounds of the clients with whom they work. This includes, but is not limited to, learning how the counselor's own cultural/ethnic/racial identity impacts values and beliefs about the counseling process."

Multicultural competency, as an ethical standard, is as important in the victim assistance profession as it is in the counseling profession. It is a skill that providers must work diligently to acquire if they are to be truly effective in their work.

Multicultural Competency in Victim Services

The development of multicultural competency in victim services requires that providers develop a basic knowledge and understanding of the races and ethnic backgrounds of those they are assisting, regardless of their culture, class, religion, spirituality, disability, gender, age, or sexual orientation. In a helping relationship with a multicultural victim, the provider should affirm the client's belief system and attempt to understand how it influences his or her life and the events and problem he or she faces.

Providers must come to understand the impact of their own race and ethnicity on their personality, communication style, values, and beliefs. Understanding their own racial orientation and identity will teach them to accept racial aspects of self and appreciate the diversity of others. It will also help them understand the influence these factors may have on a victim's behavior, interactions, and attitudes. They must also work to understand the worldviews of the victims from different cultures with which they work. This knowledge and understanding must finally be used to develop and implement culturally appropriate interventions and strategies for assisting crime victims from different cultures.

A Model for Analyzing Competency

The Multicultural Counseling Inventory (MCI) was developed in 1994 by Gargi Roysircar, Ph D., the founding director of the Antioch New England Multicultural Center for Research and Practice and leading researcher in the area of multicultural competency and clinical psychology. The MCI is a useful tool for helping providers improve their cultural competencies and evaluate their attitudes, biases, and degree of understanding of multicultural clients' realities. Modified for use by victim assistance providers, the MCI utilizes eight approaches by which providers may evaluate their ability to effectively relate to the multicultural victims they serve. Each theme represents an important knowledge area that the victim assistance provider can explore in their efforts to increase competency serving multicultural crime victims.

1. *Awareness of the minority victim's reality.* Considerations might include reflection on:

> The experience of life in a new country;
>
> The flight of political refugees and the trauma they fled;
>
> Family structure and roles; and

Victim ambivalence about participating in a helping relationship with a member of another race/culture.

2. *Self-awareness and reflection.* Consideration of the dynamics of the interpersonal relationship with the victim might include awareness of:

One's own worldview, biases, and gender attitudes;

One's own cultural diversity;

Immigration issues versus the secure status of being a U.S. citizen;

One's "privileged" status; and

One's limitations in communicating with a victim of crime who speaks another language and has a different culture, and the discomfort transmitted to the victim by "dumbing down" the exchange with simplistic speech and unnecessarily didactic explanations.

3. *Analysis of value biases.* Providers must examine their American worldview. Considerations might include:

Language use and preferences;

Family composition and structure;

Positive stereotypes about the race, ethnicity, and minority served;

Negative stereotypes about the race, ethnicity, and minority served; and

Educational status in comparison to that of the victim and how it impacts effective communication.

4. *Effectiveness of intentional exchanges of cultural information as a tool for relationship-building.* Considerations might include:

Making explicit the cultural norms of both the victim service provider and the victim;

Discussing acculturation experiences;

Discussing the victim's expectations in the helping relationship; and

Discussing religious and spiritual orientation when appropriate.

5. *Analysis of perceived barriers to effective communication.* Considerations might include:

Language difficulties;

Communication pattern differences;

Lack of up-front information about the victim's cultural background that inhibits exchange; and

Lack of understanding of the victim's goals and expectations.

6. *Victim service provider's frustration with helping relationship.* Considerations might include:

Victim service provider's distress over cultural mistakes and miscommunications; and

Inability to feel effective in the helping relationship.

7. *Analysis of difficulties generated by cultural similarities and differences.* Considerations might include:

Inappropriate assumption of similarities between the victim service provider and the victim;

Socioeconomic status differences;

Using "white society" as a point of reference; and

Making sweeping generalizations as a means to minimize differences.

8. *Anxiety about progress.* Considerations might include:

Unreasonable expectations that the victim will feel comfortable in the relationship;

Anxiety over at-risk, minority/culturally oriented behavior (e.g., loyalty to local gang or extreme passivity of women victims);

Misinterpreting missed appointments; and

Inability to address impasses.

The successful acquisition of multicultural competency allows the provider to process and gain awareness into the relative nature of "what makes sense" regarding the needs and concerns of crime victims. Going back to Sam's dilemma with the Vietnamese family, had the community-based crisis response center where he worked focused on culturally competent advocacy to the immigrant communities it served, response protocols would be in place that might avoid revictimizing the survivors because of ignorance of their customs.

Yet, Paul D. Pedersen, Ph.D., professor of psychology at the University of Hawaii and author of books and articles on multicultural counseling, offers a note of caution. No matter how culturally educated and sensitive we become, "we cannot know exactly what the client is thinking but we can assume that some of the thoughts are negative and anti-provider in their orientation. Some thoughts will be positive and pro-provider." He warns that when working to improve cultural competencies:

Oversimplifying cultural norms is a continuing risk and danger.

Looking at the opposite of what the provider believes to be true may offer surprising alternative insights from the perspective of another culture.

Providers are in greatest danger when they believe they have already discovered their biases.

Getting Clear on Roles and Responsibilities:

In absolute terms, "putting the victim first" is the top priority across all system- and community-based victim services. How providers achieve that goal, however, often depends on their job description. There are substantial differences in the kinds of services that can be delivered by system- and community-based service providers. Strengths and weaknesses inherent to each role impact how specific ethical standards are understood and acted upon.

Consider the many factors regarding confidentiality that come into play in the following scenario:

> *Mai, a university sophomore, unknowingly accepts a drink spiked with the illegal drug rohypnol from a popular young man at a fraternity party. Several hours later, Mai wakes in a bedroom and discovers she has been sexually assaulted. At first, she is ashamed and tells no one what has happened. Two days later, she realizes she has contracted an infection and goes to the university clinic. During the examination, the doctor notices signs of a forced sexual encounter. Mai tells her about the spiked drink and the assault but doesn't identify the attacker. When the tests for STDs come back positive, Mai is called back to the clinic. School policy requires that Mai reveal her partner's identity. She becomes hysterical, and the doctor calls the rape crisis clinic and asks them to send over a counselor.*

Mai desperately needs help but does not want her friends or family to learn of the victimization or the STD. How would the confidentiality standard apply to Mai during her conversation with the rape crisis counselor? Confidentiality of communications is the fundamental ethic supporting all client-provider relationships in community-based victim services. The rape crisis counselor informs Mai that all of their conversations will remain confidential. Mai is not interested in reporting the crime, and although the rape crisis counselor may disagree about the importance of a police report, she will respect Mai's wishes and not pressure her to file charges. The fact that underage alcohol and criminal drug use related to sexual assault are additional elements of the crime will be a serious concern but not a reason to report the crime to the police.

What if the doctor at the clinic calls the police when she detects signs of a sexual assault involving the criminal use of rohypnol, and a system-based advocate from law enforcement appears on the scene? How would the confidentiality standard change when the system-based provider's job is to serve and support Mai throughout the investigation process? The confidentiality of their communications would have a limited application. If Mai decides to file charges, all communications with the provider will be shared with the investigator and the district attorney, and, if relevant, be presented in court. The provider will compel Mai to reveal everything relevant to the crime. Anything important that is withheld is potentially damaging to her case. If Mai was drinking underage at the time of the crime, that condition would be considered relevant to the case and be revealed.

Learning the similarities and differences between system-based and community-based victim services is the basis for building relationships and increasing trust among providers. It is important to understand their roles and responsibilities and to whom are they ultimately accountable.

System-based Providers

Service providers working within the criminal justice system must balance the victim's interests with their other responsibilities. Their goal is to get the best possible treatment for the victim within the confines of the law and agency policy. The system advocate is accountable to the investigator or the prosecutor of the case, or to the commissioner of corrections.

System-based providers focus on:

- Victim safety
- Access to justice system information
- Right to be present and heard in court proceedings
- Restitution

System-based providers are limited in their delivery of victims' services by:

- Statutory limitations protecting offenders' rights
- Limits on confidentiality regarding victim information pertinent to the case
- Limits on support
- The duration of the case

Community-based Providers

Community-based providers, such as those working in rape crisis centers, domestic violence shelters, and homicide support groups, focus on crime victims' personal needs and concerns. Like system-based providers, community-based providers' policies and agency mandates are directed toward victim safety, victim restoration, and the effective and efficient delivery of victims' services in the system. Community-based providers are first and foremost accountable to the victim.

However, unlike system-based providers, community-based providers also deal with victims of sexual assault and domestic violence who do not report these crimes and will not use the criminal justice system as a means of addressing their victimization. In such cases, assistance to the victim may still include counseling and support during recovery from the victimization, often on a long-term basis. In addition, community-based providers educate the community about victims' rights and services and advocate for legal reform on victims' behalf.

Community-based serve crime victims exclusively by seeking the most effective means within the law for:

- Delivery of victims' rights
- Victim safety
- Victim empowerment
- Victim restoration
- Education of the community on victim needs

It is also important to keep in mind that system-based providers and community-based providers have different points of reference regarding victim assistance. For example, a community-based provider will have a broader, more encompassing point of reference than a system-based provider. This is because they must consider the full reality of victims, where and with whom they live, whether or not they can adequately take care of themselves and their families, and whether or not they have access to other community services, such as welfare housing and appropriate mental-health care. The reference point of the system-based provider is relatively short term, intrinsically tied to the criminal justice process, and includes assistance in filing a police report, court accompaniment, presenting an impact statement, applying for compensation, custody and protection concerns, meeting with prosecutors, and appearing at parole hearings.

These differing points of reference may cause conflicts between system- and community-based providers unless they have an understanding of each other's roles. Community-based providers sometimes challenge the laws and policies their system-based counterparts must uphold. They may find that their efforts to serve a victim are in conflict with system protocols. As a result, system-based providers may find their agency under attack by community-based advocates and feel divided loyalties. Therefore, two primary challenges must be faced before system- and community-based providers can come to see the logic of sharing ethical standards:

Coming to understand that their roles are complementary, not contradictory.

Coming to understand that their application of these ethical standards may differ.

Challenge 1: Complementary, not contradictory roles

A closer look at the various roles of system- and community-based providers reveals that they can have a complementary rather than adversarial relationship. The community-based provider is better placed to advocate on behalf of the victim, while the system-based provider is better placed to negotiate the system to help the victim. One of the most important challenges system- and community-based providers must overcome is the misunderstandings and mistrust generated when they find themselves working in opposition to each other to meet a victim's needs. To achieve maximum effectiveness in their service to victims, both system- and community-based providers must cultivate strong, mutually supportive, interpersonal relations by assuming that both are working with good intent, clarifying the roles each provider plays, and fostering trusting relationships.

The development of a statewide code of ethical standards that meets the needs of *both* system- and community-based providers may require an airing of the longstanding problems that have developed between the two communities. First, each group must acknowledge their common goal of putting victims first. Second, they must work together to build their relationship by clarifying their roles and responsibilities, improving their communication skills, and committing to active collaborations. Some examples of ongoing and successful enactments of this process are:

The *Community Victim Liaisons* within the Community Protection Unit at the State of Washington Department of Corrections are system-based providers who have been placed throughout the state to work with community-based providers on improving victim safety during offender reentry, sharing goals, improving accessibility, and fostering open exchange.

The *Sexual Assault Council* is an initiative in the Fairfax County, Virginia, Police Department. It is made up of community-based rape crisis counselors, law enforcement victim service providers, detectives, and high-ranking police officers (including campus police) who meet quarterly to foster better understanding of their individual roles and discuss common goals in the treatment of sexual assault victims inside and outside the agency.

The Safety Audit is an initiative developed by Praxis International and the Battered Women's Justice Project in Duluth, Minnesota, that is designed to improve coordinated community response to domestic violence cases. Part of this process has been to negotiate mutual understanding among agencies and reduce the negative impact of fragmented philosophies and response to domestic violence victims. The audit thoroughly examines agency training programs, policies, procedures, and tests, including intake forms, report formats, assessments, evaluations, checklists, and other materials, to determine if they enhance or compromise victim safety. The goal of the audit is to link what the individual practitioners do to the overall effect of the intervention.

Challenge 2: Difference in applicability of ethical standards

The second challenge is to not only recognize the value of establishing ethical standards, but to accept that their application may differ depending on the work environment of the provider. For example, confidentiality is of primary importance in community-based victim services, but may be difficult to achieve within the limitations of law or agency policy in a system-based environment.

It is clear that, while both system- and community-based providers seek to put the needs of the victim first, the nature of their roles and responsibilities vis-à-vis the victim are quite different. This does not mean that these two groups must be at odds with one another in their professional roles. Adopting an ethical code of conduct that meets the needs of both groups is in the best interests of victims.

Conclusion

The development of reliable tools for understanding and delivering ethically responsible services to crime victims begins with an assessment of the personal values and moral orientations that consciously or unconsciously influence providers' behavior. Therefore, it is important that providers take the time to assess their innate responses to personal moral dilemmas and their ability to take action when confronted with them. While personal values and professional values often stem from the same beliefs, they are different in content and should not be confused. Professional ethical standards in victim services are the rules that help make manifest the values by which providers serve crime victims and the rules that assist them in making ethical decisions. Questions over competing priorities will likely appear on a regular basis, when various options exist and choices must be made. To make choices effectively, it is critical that providers be clear about both their own values and the professional values and roles that are inherent in carrying out their professional responsibilities. Two important areas that may present ethical challenges for victim service providers—multicultural competency and conflicts between system- and community-based providers—are in need of much reflection and action.

References

Abramson, Marcia. 1996. "Reflections on Knowing Oneself Ethically: Towards a Working Framework for Social Work Practice." *Families in Society: The Journal of Contemporary Human Services* 77(4):195–201.

Arredondo, P., R. Toporek, S. Brown, J. Jones, D. Locke, J. Sanchez, and H. Stadler. 1996. "Operationalization of the Multicultural Counseling Competencies." *Journal of Multicultural Counseling and Development* 24:42–78.

Helms, J. 1984. "Towards a Theoretical Explanation of the Effects of Race on Counseling: A Black and White Model." *The Counseling Psychologist* 12(4):163–65.

Herlihy, B., and G. Corey. 1996. *ACA Ethical Standards Casebook.* 5th ed. Alexandria, Va.: American Counseling Association.

Pedersen, P. 2000. *Hidden Messages in Culture-centered Counseling: A Triad Training Model.* Thousand Oaks, Calif.: Sage.

Roysircar, G., D. Webster, J. Germer, J. Palensky, E. Lynne, G. Campbell, Y. Yang, J. Liu, and J. Blodgett-McDeavitt. 2003. "Experiential Training in Multicultural Counseling: Implementation and Evaluation of Counselor Process." In *Multicultural Competencies: A Guidebook of Practices.* Alexandria, Va.: Association for Multicultural Counseling and Development.

CHAPTER 3

Ethical Issues and Legal Concerns

Ethical dilemmas occur when conflicting values or competing priorities inhibit providers' abilities to fulfill their professional objectives on behalf of all parties concerned. Victim assistance providers may be faced with situations that involve multiple, and sometimes competing, interests. The manner in which such goals can be realized depends on the individual circumstances of each case and the degree to which competing elements require prioritization. Providers could face many ethical concerns as a result of their personal relationships with their clients. How they choose to apply their ethical standards to these situations will depend, at least to some extent, on the context of these relationships, and whether they are working in system-based services or community-based counseling and advocacy.

This chapter discusses two key ethical standards that providers must understand and abide by to maintain ethically responsible relationships with clients. Of all the ethical standards in the field of victim assistance, dual relationships and confidentiality are the most complex and multifaceted. Violation of these standards can directly harm the persons served. Liability in the delivery of services to victims is addressed by the third ethical standard discussed in this chapter, which calls for providers to understand their legal responsibilities. On one hand, noncompliance with professional rules of conduct in counseling relationships, specifically in the areas of confidentiality, duty to warn, informed consent, and confidential privilege, has legal consequences. Protection from liability in the delivery of services to crime victims and unauthorized practice of law are also topics of increasing significance. This chapter explores all of these themes. *Note: Because new state laws are passed and court decisions are filed that impact the field, practitioners are strongly encouraged to educate themselves and remain up to date on their state laws and recent court decisions as part of their ethical competency.*

Dual Relationships and Boundaries

Ethical Standard 3.8: The victim assistance provider does not engage in personal relationships with persons served which exploit professional trust or which could impair the victim assistance provider's objectivity and professional judgment.

If providers offer friendship to victims outside the purview of their duties, or if they exchange goods and services with victims, then professional boundaries have been violated and a dual relationship has been created. In a counseling or advocacy relationship, the provider has professional influence over the victim. When a second or dual relationship is established, the provider's influence and the victim's subordination are generally replicated. The victim remains vulnerable to the provider's position of power, creating an unfair dynamic in the second relationship. This blurring of the boundaries between the primary and secondary relationships permits the abuse of power.

Engaging in a sexual relationship with a victim while in counseling has been likened to the dynamics of incest in terms of the power to exploit. Yet even providers' well-intentioned actions in the offering of friendships may constitute breaches of professional boundaries and therefore have potential for causing harm. Anytime providers venture outside the boundaries established in the professional code of ethics, they do a disservice to the victim, who may ultimately experience distrust and anger. See the examples below in which different boundaries have been crossed, some of which appear to be harmless:

> A college student becomes enamored with her counselor after he meets her for lunch at the school cafeteria and she misunderstands his intentions.

> A domestic violence victim assistance provider gives her home phone number to a battered woman who is particularly fragile and finds the victim's angry batterer on her own front porch a week later.

A victim assistance provider lies to her boss about the extent of her personal friendship with a member of her empowerment counseling group instead of revealing that she has been babysitting on weekends for the victim's three children.

A counselor for families who have lost loved ones to vehicular homicide knows that one of the participants in her support group is the wife of her husband's boss.

The issue of self-disclosure is also important in a discussion of boundary issues. Many providers have experienced a victimization in their past that has motivated them to help others to heal. The urge to self-disclose, to establish common ground, and to demonstrate a deeper level of empathy should always be questioned. Victims in counseling relationships must be allowed the emotional space to focus on their own issues.

Victim assistance providers who enter into dual relationships with victims often rationalize their behavior by asserting that the circumstances are unique. Or, they insist that they cannot serve the client without making tremendous efforts that exceed normal boundaries. "Over-helping" is another aspect of dual relationships. Regardless of these well-meaning intentions, crossing the boundaries of ethical practice creates a potentially exploitive situation for the victim and impairs the good judgment of the provider.

Yet, dual relationships in small communities are almost impossible to avoid. The only available advocate or care provider may be a relative or a close friend of the victim or the offender. This is often the case in indigenous, immigrant, and rural communities and within groups of people with a shared trait such as the gay, lesbian, bisexual, and transgender community or the deaf and hard of hearing. Equally difficult is the avoidance of exchange of goods and services in small communities where the poverty level is high. Refusal to provide services to an individual, with whom one has another relationship in either of these circumstances, would be a violation of the ethic of putting the victim first (see Ethical Standard 3.2). Therefore, the provider must be especially diligent to respect the purpose of each of the boundary themes listed in the following paragraph. It is important to recognize that even though there may be variances in the dual relationship code in small communities, boundary ethics can be adhered to.

The Pennsylvania Coalition Against Rape (PCAR) discusses the importance of setting and maintaining boundaries in *The Trainer's Toolbox:*

A Resource Guide for Sexual Assault Counselor Training. This book, which is used widely as a training resource among providers that counsel victims, emphasizes four important purposes served by professional boundaries:

1. *Boundaries* safely and effectively designate and preserve times, places, spaces, relationships, ideas, and people for a specific purpose.

2. *Boundaries* provide a dedicated space, place, relationship, or agreement devoted to protecting what is vulnerable and safeguarding what is valuable.

3. *Boundaries* in relationships keep us faithful to the purpose of the relationship.

4. *Boundaries* make it possible for us to safely venture into relationships of trust and vulnerability.

These four purposes are critical to the provider-victim relationship. Failure to respect them can cause considerable harm to the victim. If providers engage in dual relationships or have an inclination to do so, they should seek assistance in identifying their motivations, and request intensive supervision of their interactions with victims. If necessary, they may need to leave their job until the ability to maintain appropriate boundaries has been reestablished.

Confidentiality

Ethical Standard 3.5: The victim assistance provider preserves the confidentiality of information provided by the person served or acquired from other sources before, during, and after the course of the professional relationship.

The victim's right to confidential communications with the service provider is a professional ethical standard that is essential to the successful development of a helping, trusting relationship.

> Sophie is in a counseling session with Ricardo and Leeza Romano, who have lost their only son in a homicide and are trying to save their marriage. When Ricardo leaves the room to make a telephone call, Leeza tells Sophia that her husband beats her when he is angry. Then Leeza asks the counselor not to disclose her confidence.

What should Sophie do in this situation? Confidentiality is the foundation from which trust in the provider-victim relationship is developed and nurtured. Serving victims often requires that providers become involved in private and personal areas of people's lives. Respecting the privacy of the victims served and keeping all aspects of the relationship confidential to the fullest extent possible is an ethic that applies to every client served. Many providers are required to sign confidentiality agreements with their agencies. They are also required to maintain the confidentiality of agency records and are held accountable for adherence to the agency policy on confidentiality.

Exceptions to Confidentiality

In some situations, confidentiality can, and even should, be broken. Therefore it is the provider's duty to inform a victim of these exceptions at the beginning of the relationship (except in extraordinary crisis situations). Exceptions to the right of confidentiality include the following circumstances:

Emergency health issues (including death), e.g., information pertaining to the health of an individual in need of immediate medical intervention;

Conditions relating to minor victims, e.g., reports of abuse and/ or imminent danger to the minor;

Sharing of information among agency colleagues that extends the confidentiality clause to those privy to the information;

Confidential communications that reveal threats of imminent harm to clients or third parties; and

Court orders requiring advocates to testify.

In many states, providers will also be mandated to report elder abuse. During a confidential communication, if the client reveals serious abuse of a family member who is an elderly person, it will be both the provider's right and duty to reveal the abuse to adult protective services.

Duty to Warn

Duty to warn is the legal obligation to inform people of danger and becomes relevant when a victim makes serious threats to harm someone during a confidential communication. The duty to warn exception to the right of confidentiality fosters ethical dilemmas when the need to safeguard the right of confidentiality conflicts with the need to prevent harm to individuals.

> *Jerry was sexually abused by his wrestling coach in grade school and he never told anyone. Since he disclosed his victimization during therapy sessions with Frank, his counselor, Jerry has repeatedly threatened to "beat the man silly" if he could find him. Two weeks ago, the coach was arrested and charged with the sexual molestation of a child. He has been released on bail from the city jail and Jerry is on the lookout for him. No one else knows that Jerry has been molested, and Frank realizes that if he discloses the threat to the coach and this information becomes public, Jerry will be traumatized.*

The precedent for the "duty to warn and protect third parties" exception in the field of psychotherapy was set by the U.S. Supreme Court in 1976 in the landmark case of *Tarasoff v. Regents of the University of California.* In this case, a therapist at the university health center failed to warn a female student that her ex-boyfriend had made threats against her life during his counseling sessions. The ex-boyfriend later stabbed the female student to death. The decision cited four conditions that were necessary for the duty to warn exception to be acted upon in a counseling relationship:

- There should be evidence that the client presents a threat of violence to another.
- The violent act must be foreseeable.
- The violent act must be impending.
- The counselor must be able to identify a potential victim.

Underlying the confusion regarding confidentiality and duty to warn is the need for victim service providers and agencies to clearly distinguish between what they are required to do by law in their state and what is an adopted ethical guideline or policy for the profession and/or their organization.

Informed Consent

In the context of confidentiality, *informed consent* refers to a written release signed by the victim that permits providers to disclose written or oral communications to any individual or entity. For the consent to be truly *informed*, the victim should have a thorough understanding of the reason and the impact of both disclosure and nondisclosure on his or her well-being and life circumstances.

> *Soledad confides to her domestic violence advocate, Maria, that she needs help to deal with her drinking problem. She is afraid to attend Alcoholics Anonymous meetings because her husband might find out and use it against her in the upcoming custody battle for their three children. Maria plans a strategy with Soledad to attain the treatment she requires without jeopardizing her status as a competent mother for her children. To get her into an affordable private program where her identity would be better protected, Maria needs to make the referral on Soledad's behalf. Maria asks Soledad to sign a statement giving her consent to intervene on her behalf for substance abuse treatment. Maria explains to Soledad that there is a good chance that her husband will not find out about her participation in the private program but there is no guarantee, and that she should weigh the importance of getting immediate treatment against the reduced risks of a disclosure to her husband about her problem.*

Five factors should be present for an informed consent to qualify as an exception to confidentiality in the field of victim assistance:

1. *Disclosure of information.* Maria, with Soledad's consent, will disclose to a private substance abuse treatment program through a professional referral that Soledad requires their services.

2. *Understanding of the information.* Maria must clearly explain the pros and cons of Soledad's participation in the treatment program. Her informed consent is required to breach the confidentiality standard so Maria can help her gain access to the affordable program.

3. *Voluntariness of consent.* Maria cannot force Soledad to sign the informed consent by use of threats or intimidation.

4. *Competence to consent.* When Maria explains the meaning and

purpose of the informed consent and when Soledad signs it, Soledad has to be clear-headed and responsible for her actions. For Soledad to sign the document while under the influence of alcohol would violate the intention of the informed consent exception to confidentiality.

5. *Clear time frame for which the consent is valid.* The more specific the time frame of the informed consent and the content of the information to be shared, the more likely it will be that Maria's confidential privilege over communications with Soledad will be protected in court. Opened ended informed consent documents are vulnerable to court subpoenas.

Maria should also explain to Soledad that treatment providers are subject to the Code of Federal Regulations (42 U.S.C. 290dd-2) that protect individuals in recovery from dissemination of information about their diagnosis, treatment, and referral for treatment under Confidentiality of Alcohol and Drug Abuse Patient Records.

Confidential Privilege

Confidential privilege refers to legal rights of confidentiality, such as attorney-client privilege or the psychotherapist-patient privilege. In a courtroom, the privilege permits the client/patient to "own" the information that has been communicated to the lawyer/psychotherapist. Only the client/patient may *waive* the privilege, which gives consent to revealing the information in court.

Confidential privilege is not a *guaranteed right* in the field of victim services. It is however, a valuable right and one that is helpful to victim service providers who counsel and support crime victims. For example, in the case of crisis response where a provider may unintentionally become party to information that would reflect badly on a victim in court or in a counseling relationship where a victim reveals information that he or she want to remain private, the right of privilege protects the confidentiality of the information or communication.

Laws in some states have extended the right of confidential privilege to domestic violence and sexual assault service providers to protect communications with the victims they serve. This is generally specific and governed by restrictions such as the following excerpt from Colorado Statutes 13-90-107, *Who May Not Testify in Court*:

> (k)(I) A victim's advocate shall not be examined as to any communication made to such victim's advocate by a victim of domestic violence as defined by sections . . .

or a victim of sexual assault, as described in sections . . . , in person or through the media of written records or reports without the consent of the victim.

(II) For purposes of this paragraph (k), a "victim's advocate" means a person at a battered women's shelter or rape crisis organization or a comparable community-based advocacy program for victims of domestic violence or sexual assault and does not include an advocate employed by any law enforcement agency:

(A) Whose primary function is to render advice, counsel, or assist victims of domestic or family violence or sexual assault; and

(B) Who has undergone not less than fifteen hours of training as a victim's advocate or, with respect to an advocate who assists victims of sexual assault, not less than thirty hours of training as a sexual assault victim's advocate; and

(C) Who supervises employees of the program, administers the program, or works under the direction of a supervisor of the program.

The question over confidential privilege between providers and victims in a counseling relationship is addressed somewhat differently in Pennsylvania.

The Pennsylvania statue regarding "Confidential Communications to Sexual Assault Counselors" specifically prohibits the sexual assault counselor from consenting to be examined in any civil or criminal proceeding (regarding the confidential communications) without the written consent of the victim. Furthermore, this absolute privilege to the sexual assault counselor prohibits the police, the district attorney, and/or their detectives from talking to the counselor and prohibits the defense attorney from requesting information.

Confidentiality protection within the Pennsylvania Protection from Abuse Act provides that:

Unless the victim waives the privilege in a signed writing prior to testimony or disclosure, a domestic violence counselor/advocate or co-participant who is present during domestic violence counseling/advocacy shall not be competent nor permitted to testify or to otherwise disclose confidential communications made to or by the counselor to the victim. The privilege shall terminate upon the death of the victim. Neither the domestic violence counselor/advocate nor the victim shall waive the privilege of confidential communications by reporting facts of physical or sexual assault under a Federal or State mandatory reporting statute or a local mandatory reporting ordinance.

Community-based legal advocates who work with victims of domestic violence and sexual assault stress the importance of working to ensure the confidential privilege remains absolute. If ever the privilege is qualified and the advocate is required to testify, practically speaking, the privilege disappears because it permits the judge to decide what evidence is relevant to the case. To meet their own ethical obligations in ensuring that the privilege of confidentiality is safeguarded, providers should defend the confidential privilege with great care, and work to ensure, as much as is feasible, that any required waivers on the privilege are as narrow and specific as they can be, and, if possible, have a specific time limitation or deadline imposed.

A U.S. Supreme Court case, *Jaffe v. Redmond*, 518 U.S. 1 (1996), offers some hope for extending the psychotherapist-patient privilege to other counseling relationships. This case held that the conversations and notes of a social worker who was counseling a police officer sued for civil rights violations were protected from legal discovery under the psychotherapist-patient privilege. However, this case has been interpreted in a number of ways by a number of courts and is not considered a precedent for extending this type of protection to the victim assistance provider–client relationship. Indeed, part of the rationale in the *Jaffe* decision is to provide lower-income individuals who seek counseling in the less-expensive relationship afforded by clinical social workers the same types of protections afforded to those who can afford to see a psychotherapist.

Remaining up to date on state laws about confidentiality issues and recent court decisions should be considered part of ethical competency. In their individual states, providers should determine if their ethical code on confidentiality is supported with existing state law on confidential privilege.

Legal Responsibilities and Liabilities

Ethical Standard 1.1: The victim assistance provider understands his or her legal responsibilities, limitations, and the implications of his/her actions within the service delivery setting and performs duties in accord with laws, regulations, policies, and legislated rights of persons served.

As the victim assistance discipline evolves and performance standards become institutionalized, civil liability concerns assume greater importance. The question of what kind of legal liability is incurred by victim assistance providers in the course of their daily responsibilities is not easily answered. Little established statutory or case law is directly applicable to victim assistance providers in terms of legal liability. Issues being addressed on the state and federal level are beginning to lay the groundwork for greater protection from liability and for confidential privilege, but the issues are still largely unlitigated and applied differently in different states. Therefore, providers and their agencies should be as educated as possible about state and federal statutes relevant to their liability in the course of their professional duties. Most agencies and organizations are aware of the applicable statutes; if not, victim advocates may need to address the issue with supervisors and research applicable laws and regulations.

In addition to confidential privilege, there are two areas of legal obligations about which victim assistance providers should educate themselves: protection from civil liability, and unauthorized practice of law, legal advocacy versus legal advice

Protection from Civil Liability

Generally speaking, service providers that are paid staff at system- and community-based victim service organizations are protected from civil liability by their employer's liability insurance. A few states, however, have passed laws to grant specific immunity from liability to victim service providers. For example, following a violent incident that occurred on the premises of a domestic violence shelter that received national attention in 2001, Ohio passed a landmark law that grants immunity from civil liability to shelter staff. At the 2001–2 session of the Ohio General Assembly, SB 131 was passed to grant two distinct immunities from civil liability to domestic violence shelters and their directors, owners, trustees, officers, victim advocates, and volunteers.

The first section of law addresses liability for harm caused by a perpetrator that entered the shelter premises illegally, remained on the premises illegally, entered the premises under a false identity, or entered the premises but did not appear to pose a threat to the shelter client or any other person on the premises. Such immunity is not available to the shelter or shelter staff if the plaintiff in the civil action can establish that an action or omission involved bad faith, or that reckless conduct contributed to the harm sustained by individuals on the shelter premises. Release of confidential information pertaining to the shelter client is considered reckless conduct.

The second immunity granted to the shelter and the shelter staff protects from civil liability for harm caused to a shelter client on premises other than the shelter when the shelter staff member is providing assistance, including but not limited to a healthcare practitioner or attorney's offices. The immunity is not available if the shelter staff has demonstrated reckless conduct or bad faith that directly contributed to the harm caused.

Volunteer staff members are protected from civil liability by the Volunteer Protection Act and state Good Samaritan laws. The Volunteer Protection Act of 1997 grants volunteers who work for not-for-profit organizations immunity from personal liability. Under P.L. 105-19, volunteer victim assistance providers, such as hotline counselors and shelter staff who work without monetary compensation, have legal protection from civil liability. This preempts state laws that offer less protection, establishing a minimum standard of protection if the individuals:

- Acted in the scope of their volunteer activity.
- Were appropriately certified by the organization and their activities were undertaken within the scope of their volunteer responsibilities.
- Were not exhibiting willful or criminal misconduct, gross negligence, or reckless behavior.
- Were not driving a motor vehicle, vessel, or aircraft at the time that the harm was caused.

The Volunteer Protection Act also requires that nonprofit organizations engaging volunteers adhere to risk management procedures that include mandatory training for volunteers. The limitations on liability protection to volunteers include harm caused by crimes of violence, hate crimes, sexual offenses, violation of a civil rights law, and harm caused while under the influence of alcohol or drugs.

Other protections from liability for volunteers include indemnification of volunteers by the association, association liability insurance that covers volunteers, and state Good Samaritan laws. They typically offer protection from liability to individuals who render emergency care for free and in good faith. They were first created to protect medical doctors from liability for their treatment of injured parties in automobile accidents and natural disasters. Many states have extended their Good Samaritan laws to protect volunteers from liability.

Unauthorized Practice of Law: Legal Advocacy versus Legal Advice

Legal advocacy to crime victims is complicated by unauthorized practice of law (UPL) statutes. Many victims of domestic violence pursue cases in court for custody and restraining orders without the services of a lawyer, and legal advocates often find themselves walking a fine line between assisting victims in the legal process and UPL. All states have laws that limit the practice of law to licensed attorneys, but the courts differ widely on how they enforce the law. Generally, the courts look at UPL in terms of harm caused by the practice of law by an unlicensed person. Community-based organizations that offer legal advocacy to crime victims should develop strict guidelines for their providers to avoid charges of UPL.

Project Safeguard, a legal advocacy organization with offices in several counties in Colorado, clearly conveys in their mission statement that they "offer insight into the legal process in the civil and criminal courts," working "to empower domestic violence survivors by supplying information, emotional support, referrals and resources," but they do not give legal advice. For the many clients who cannot afford legal services and must represent themselves, Project Safeguard offers "how-to" clinics for temporary and permanent restraining orders and divorce/custody procedures. The following is an excerpt from Project Safeguard's training for legal advocates:

> As legal advocates, we must constantly be aware of not crossing the boundary of giving legal advice, or engaging in the unauthorized practice of law. Although

not precisely defined, legal advice is generally applying legal statutes to a person's individual circumstances, or applying to a particular set of facts to the law. Advice in general is defined as opinion offered to influence another's course of action—something any good counselor should avoid anyway! However, this can be very difficult to remember when a battered woman is sitting in front of you, saying, "What should I do?"

In circumstances where a service provider offers support to a victim who has legal questions, it is always useful to consider the core principles of empowerment counseling before responding.

- Present them with options.
- Support them but don't tell them what to do.
- Explain protocols and procedures but don't try to predict specific outcomes.

In the case of legal advocacy, the role of the victim assistance provider is to:

- Inform victims of the range of legal options available to them.
- Help victims assess the pros and cons of actions they may choose to take and potential outcomes.
- Explain legal terminology and the court process.
- Help victims prepare their arguments to the judge so that they make their intentions clear.

Conclusion

Relationships with crime victims in a professional setting, particularly those that involve care, support, and counseling, can be problematic if the provider is unclear about the importance of maintaining correct boundaries. The ethical guidelines for avoiding dual relationships in victim services are designed to decrease the risk of breaches, and it is important that providers be vigilant in enforcing them. Confidentiality is an ethical standard of fundamental importance for building relationships of trust, as well as a debated area of the law. It is incumbent upon both providers and the agencies for which they work to learn their state statutes with respect to confidentiality and its exceptions. One important exception is the duty to warn, an area of law that is not consistently applied. Informed consent guidelines describe the manner in which a provider must approach a victim for permission to release information gathered from confidential communications in order to benefit the victim's case or help the victim access services. Providers should become aware of potential legal liabilities they face in the delivery of services to victims; and they should understand how they are protected from legal liability by their agencies and state statutes. The provider/client relationship issues raised in this chapter are arguably the cornerstone of the delivery of ethical victim assistance.

References

Greenhouse, L. 1996. "Justices Recognize Confidential Privilege Between Therapist and Patient." *New York Times*, June 14. <http://www.nytimes.com.96/14/6/front/scotus.privilege.html>

Jaffe v. Redmond, 518 U.S. 1 (1996).

Kagle, J., and P. Giebelhausen. 1994. "Dual Relationships and Professional Boundaries." *Social Work* 39(2): 213–19.

Lewis, H. 1982. *The Intellectual Base of Social Work Practice*. New York: Hawarth Press.

Manning, S., and C. Gaul. 1997. "The Ethics of Informed Consent." *Social Work in Health Care* 25(3):103–17.

Nelken, M. Winter 2000. "The Limits of Privilege: The Developing Scope of Federal Psychotherapist-Patient Privilege Law." *The Review of Litigation* 20(1). <http://jaffee-redmond.org/articles/nelken.htm>

Pennsylvania Coalition Against Rape (PCAR). 2000. *The Trainer's Toolbox: A Resource Guide for Sexual Assault Counselor Training*, 369–74. Harrisburg: Pennsylvania Department of Public Welfare.

Project Safeguard. 2002. Volunteer Training Manual. Denver: Not published.

Reamer, F. 1998. *Ethical Standards in Social Work: A Critical Review of the NASW Code of Ethics*. Washington, D.C.: NASW Press.

Rock, B., and E. Congress. 1999. *The New Confidentiality for the 21st Century in a Managed Care Environment*. Washington, D.C.: NASW Press.

Tarasoff v. Regents of the University of California. 551 P.2d 334 (1976).

Legislation

Colorado H.B. 95-1070. §2, 13-90-107 (3). *Who may not testify without consent*. June 3, 1995.

42 Pa. C.S.A. §5945. I. Confidential Communications to Sexual Assault Counselors, as amended 1190, Dec. P/L/737 no. 183 §1.

Ohio S.B. 131. 124th General Assembly, August 14, 2002.

23 Pa. C.S. §§6101 et seq., Pennsylvania Protection from Abuse Act, as amended 5/11/2000. §6116.

U.S. Public Law 105-19. 105th Cong., June 18, 1997. *The Volunteer Protection Act of 1997.*

CHAPTER 4

Managing Ethical Dilemmas

The practical application of professional ethical standards is not clear-cut when circumstances involve multiple interests and perspectives. When a question arises as to what is the most ethical course of professional conduct in a particular situation, an ethical "dilemma" may exist. A dilemma suggests that the answer is not obvious; there may be more than one "right" answer for the situation, depending on the various interests of the parties involved. These issues may be so complex that arriving at a clear and ethical course of action becomes a difficult process—and may be further complicated by common pitfalls in the resolution process. This chapter explores the concept of an ethical dilemma, false dilemmas, common obstacles to the resolution of dilemmas, and strategies for resolving dilemmas.

Are Ethical Challenges Always Dilemmas?

Some ethical standards are simply rules that must be followed. For example, victim service providers must accurately represent their titles and qualifications. They must also provide full information about fees or financial information pertinent to services for victims. These ethical standards are quite straightforward.

When a combination of ethical issues arises in the delivery of services to a victim, adherence to standards must be prioritized based on the needs of the person served, agency policy, and state law. Moreover, services to victims that involve multiple providers may present situations where ethical priorities differ; for example, a domestic violence counselor might have a stronger commitment to the right of self-determination than a service provider in a police department. Neither of the above situations necessarily results in an ethical dilemma. Problems are likely to arise, however, when the ethical standards conflict and the interpretations of the situation are limited by both the personalities and the motivations of everyone involved.

In *A Practical Companion to Ethics*, Anthony Weston, a professor of philosophy at Oxford University, creates a useful construct to: 1) discuss barriers to problem solving before situations become ethical dilemmas; 2) apply techniques to prevent ethical dilemmas if they do arise; and 3) avoid mental attitudes that inhibit the possibility of thoughtful awareness in the resolution of ethical dilemmas.

Two attitudes inevitably limit the resolution of ethical issues: the creation of false dilemmas; and rigid patterns of thinking. *False dilemmas* occur when the options for resolving a situation become unnecessarily limited (typically to two), creating an either/or situation. In this situation, one of the two options becomes defined as necessarily "right," while the other is necessarily "wrong." When faced with an either/or situation, providers should try asking themselves and others how they can expand their options.

For example, the discovery of child neglect that requires immediate removal from the home against the victims' will could be a false dilemma. The removal issue becomes the either/or situation and the limited thinking that sets up the false dilemma only permits two options: the neglected remain in the home where they continue to be harmed, or they are removed to foster care where they are safe (but possibly extremely unhappy).

Another (ineffective) approach to problem solving that limits options is *rigid patterns of thinking*, which tend to dominate reasoning based on what has worked in the past and is therefore comfortable. Sometimes the stress caused by an ethical dilemma can result in a defensive attitude that limits the provider's ability to think expansively, or causes the provider to be reluctant to venture outside his or her regular pool of advisors and gather new perspectives: "We have always done it that way." Additionally, a provider's perspective may become limited by preset attitudes developed over years of working in the victim assistance field. When faced with a seemingly impossible dilemma, a victim assistance provider may find it useful to consult professionals in unrelated fields for a fresh analysis of the situation (if there are no confidentiality considerations that would prevent this).

Weston suggests that the most appropriate solutions are always found in the most effective framing of problems. Brainstorming, reframing problems, and preventative ethics are three approaches that victim assistance providers can apply to arrive at more options:

1. *Brainstorm* with a group of colleagues to generate new options. Successful brainstorming requires discussing every suitable option, even if it is only remotely possible. This is because even discussions of options that turn out to be unsuitable may trigger a more suitable idea.

Consider the neglected children who have been removed from their home against their will. Through brainstorming with colleagues, a provider may find others means to remedy the neglect so that the children can stay with their parent(s). Assistance from other family members and relatives, after-school care, and/or support through faith-based organizations may all be options that could relieve pressure and allow the parent(s) time to make the home safe and healthy.

2. *Reframe the problem.* Reframing a problem can change the dynamics of the issue and allow a provider to explore more options. Are the causes that provoke the dilemma part of a larger process that can be modified to positively impact the situation or to eliminate it entirely?

There may be correlating factors to the neglect that can be addressed to improve the care of the children in the home. Perhaps the children are neglected because the single mother, who is ineligible for welfare and works two back-to-back jobs, is unable to care for them properly. Her time is spent trying to pay the rent, pay for their food, and clothe them. Assistance to the mother may be the best way to address neglect of the children. In other words, are the causes of the dilemma symptoms or root causes of the overall problem?

3. *Use preventive ethics.* Preventive ethics take the approach that often-times ethical dilemmas result from injustice or the application of limited options in another context that should and could be remedied directly.

> *Angie is a victim of a violent crime with severe physical injuries who was ordered restitution by the courts. Since Caleb, the offender, was sentenced to prison for several years, no action was taken on the restitution order. However, the*

parole board ordered that Caleb begin making restitution payments upon release as a condition of his supervision. When Angie received notification that Caleb had been released, she contacted the local parole office to ask about her payments. The parole officer was slow to respond.

A year later, before any action was taken, Caleb broke his back at work and retired on his employer's liability insurance. At that point, his parole officer believed that it would be unethical to require him to pay restitution in his injured condition. Looking for a settlement and a piece of his insurance money, Angie got in touch with victim services at the parole office to advocate for her. The negotiation within the agency soon reached an impasse.

Preventive ethics would take the approach that the ethical dilemma over Caleb's ability to pay restitution in his injured condition results from a prior injustice: the failure of the supervisor to enforce the parole board's order to pay Angie upon his release. If the paroling authority had an established policy to see that restitution obligations were honored, the ethical dilemma would have been prevented. The restitution could have been paid before the accident occurred, at least in part, and there would have been some sense that the criminal justice system had held Caleb directly accountable to Angie for some of the harm caused.

When ethical dilemmas *are* unavoidable, finding an effective resolution to the ethical issues will require thoughtful consideration and patience. When attempting to resolve ethical dilemmas it is important to:

1. Find out the details of the case in terms of who will be affected and place it in context.

2. Ask the following questions: Who is facing the dilemma? Who will be most affected by the resolution? What are the options for resolution? What will be the criteria for decision-making?

3. Look at the moral problem from other perspectives in enough detail to understand the opposing logic and the impact the resolution of the dilemma will have on others.

4. Seek to understand the opponents' position. Treat opponents as friends, look for the merits of their arguments, and reexamine positions in order to address their concerns.

5. Consider the abstract concepts that bear upon the situation (i.e.,

justice, evil, equality), and how they are understood within the community.

6. Look for the ethical codes that apply to the situation in their cultural context. Are there contradictions among codes?

The resolution of ethical dilemmas challenges feelings. Most providers working in victim services have a passion for justice and a remarkable capacity for empathy. Their feelings are powerful energizing forces that drive them to work tirelessly on behalf of victims. However, while their instinctive reactions will be their first indication of the fairness or unfairness of a situation that involves an ethical concern, they must analyze all the components of a dilemma. Weston proposes three mental attitudes that inhibit or eliminate the possibility of thoughtful awareness in the resolution of ethical dilemmas: dogmatism, rationalization, and relativism.

Dogmatism is the assertion of strong opinions on a subject often without reference to evidence. People who are dogmatic are committed to fixed principles and try to live up to those principles. They believe that having doubts about moral positions is wishy-washy or weak. People who are dogmatic stand in the way of ethical reasoning by opposing any argument or attack on their position by dismissing it without reflection. By definition, ethical dilemmas occur when values come into conflict. A dogmatic person's refusal to reflect on the opposing party's position creates an impasse. Any mindfulness dedicated to ethical reasoning is stifled. The extent of dogmatism expressed by any individual may be all encompassing or occur in a limited fashion on a single topic. Those who have fought intense uphill battles for a cause can be somewhat polarized in their attitudes, and dogmatic thinking may inhibit their efforts to resolve ethical challenges.

Rationalizations occur when people want to assert their ideas or justify their actions but lack plausible-sounding reasons to back up their positions. They may just feel or want to believe that their position is the right one. Rationalizations are a defensive tactic intended to avoid embarrassment or anger when people are faced with their own lack of information or uncertainty. People tend to rationalize over issues where they feel unprepared to defend a position. When employed in the resolution of ethical dilemmas, rationalization is a self-defeating tactic because it is easily challenged, wastes time and energy, and tries the patience of the other participants in the discussion.

Relativism is a point of view from which a conclusion is drawn in which no single standard is right or wrong because all values and systems of ethical belief differ according to people, circumstance, and cultures. This approach can be entirely appropriate in the cultivation of the open-minded receptivity and understanding required to cultivate diversity and tolerance. However, it can also become a way to avoid tackling an ethical dilemma by inhibiting the critical thinking required to analyze the issues at stake. Agreeing to disagree is a careless and potentially harmful response to an ethical challenge, particularly when resolution of the dilemma will affect the well-being of others.

In addition to the three inhibiting factors suggested by Weston, *passivity* is another mental attitude that hampers the resolution of ethical dilemmas. Oddly enough, *passion* and *passivity* share the same root word in classical Latin, *passus* (to endure). Yet, modern usage defines *passion* as having deep feelings for and an eagerness to pursue a person or cause. Passivity, on the other hand, has retained much of its original meaning— to be acted upon without exerting influence or acting in return. Moral passivity in general has contributed to widespread victimization in communities, in nations, and throughout the world. Domestic violence, slavery, and genocide are all issues about which many people have remained passive until too many lives have been destroyed or lost. Indeed, passivity in face of grave moral issues is complicity.

Cultivating awareness of mental attitudes that inhibit the resolution of ethical dilemmas is an essential practice. Yet, being open-hearted in the resolution of an ethical dilemma is just as important as being open-minded. Relating positively with those on the opposite side of the discussion rather than objectifying them as the "enemy" enhances the possibility of a creative interaction. Communication should be respectful, open-hearted, and appropriate to the cultural context of the ethical dilemma.

Dilemmas and Effective Communication

Victim assistance providers should be guided by principles of respect, integrity, and social justice when they engage in problem-solving dialogues to resolve issues within or outside their agencies. Ethical communication is a standard for professional conduct that applies to all aspects of the victim services discipline and is a particularly useful and desirable skill when it comes to discussing professional values in conflict.

Good communication skills may take a lifetime to develop, but it is important that providers always attempt to articulate their views clearly, are able to hear another's viewpoint, and can disagree in a way that is respectful and direct. Providers should ask themselves:

Am I a good listener?

Do I hear other points of view before beginning to edit comments and form rebuttals?

Am I motivated by winning or by finding the best solution for everyone involved?

Do I work to create a safe environment where participants are able to speak freely, challenge each other, and share new ideas?

The following material has been adapted from "A Feminist Perspective on the Ethics of Communication," a study by Kit Evans, executive director of the AWAKE Shelter in Boulder, Colorado. The study was appended and expanded in 1998 by Lisa Olcese and Lisa Calderon of the Safehouse Progressive Alliance for Nonviolence, Inc., as a document entitled *Ethical Communication: A Method of Social Transformation*. These guidelines were developed to help victim assistance providers improve their communication skills within their organizations:

1. *Agendas and goals to be accomplished.*

   Personal agendas are valid when they are shared with the group. Sharing promotes group cohesiveness and inclusion of everyone's ideas.

   Secret agendas or withholding information and opinions can be dishonest and divisive.

   People have a right to information that affects them, particularly during times of conflict.

   No true group decision can be reached if one segment of its members manipulates, misinforms, or under-informs another.

2. *Avoidance of oppressive behavior and silencing.*

   Put-downs, verbal attacks, threats, and innuendo are unethical means of directly silencing others.

   Teasing, minimizing, interrupting, and nonverbal communication are unethical means of *indirectly* silencing others.

Oppressive words and actions result in power over another, and cause distress, alienation, and disempowerment and deny the group the benefit of valuable input.

People who feel that they were not allowed input will have no investment in upholding the decision.

3. *Honesty and individual responsibility.*

Providers must understand their personal triggers, and be accountable for their words, actions, and judgments.

Anger can be positive, but the dialogue should not be used to vent personal problems.

The goal is to create a positive, well-functioning environment built on strong relationships and openness to different perspectives.

4. *Respect for everyone.*

Participants should never be marginalized because of different levels of power within the group.

Everyone has the responsibility to create a safe environment.

5. *Commitment to resolving the conflict.*

Discuss what resolution will look like.

6. *Focus on specific sources of concern.*

Avoid placing people in the middle of conflicts that do not concern them. Avoid gossip and group fragmentation.

7. *Clarity of point of view.*

Use "I" statements, clear language, and as many specific examples as possible.

8. *Sufficient time to work through the problem.*

When the resolution cannot be attained in the first encounter, make a commitment to ongoing discussion.

9. *Openness to new ideas.*

Constructive criticism is ethical. Disagreement is healthy.

10. *Recognition of "unearned privileges" as a result of gender, class, and race.*

Privileges might affect the ability to communicate effectively and clearly.

Privileges that remain unexamined create the risk of carrying biases, assumptions, and expectations that can lead to oppression.

In 2004, the Denver Victim Services Network (VSN) formulated a Conflict Resolution Process based on the Victim Services 2000 ethical standard that addresses ethical communication. Part 3, Section of the Code of Ethics, calls for victim assistance providers to "seek appropriate methods for addressing conflict that will model constructive conflict resolution processes when conflict with colleagues arises." The VSN Conflict Resolution Process is presented in the appendix of this text.

Ethical Decision-Making

Ethical decisions should be made in a systematic and logical way that recognizes that there are multiple points of view in most dilemmas. Circumstances requiring ethical decisions are rarely clear-cut, and they generally involve numerous interests and competing obligations. Many ethical decision-making models exist that can be useful for analyzing and resolving ethical dilemmas in victim services. Most of them are six- to eight-step processes that require:

1. Assessment of the facts;

2. Identification of the relevant ethical standards;

3. Assessment of the practical concerns that impact the decision-making process;

4. Consideration of the possible courses of action;

5. Consideration of the consequences of the possible courses of action;

6. Consultation with a peer or a supervisor;

7. Selection of the best option and action; and

8. Evaluation of the outcomes.

A short version of the six- to eight-step ethical decision-making model is presented below and can serve as a tool to help readers systematically analyze a dilemma from all points of view and then project possible outcomes in hopes of arriving at the best possible resolution.

The following case study is intentionally complex and presents several related ethical dilemmas that should be analyzed from all angles to arrive at an informed ethical decision.

> *Yvonne is an advocate at Financial Crimes Unit in the district attorney's office. Joe and Alice Carson were recently victims of a costly credit-card scam. Yvonne was asked to help them limit their financial losses. Alice Carson, 46, works at a dry cleaning establishment and her husband Joe, 58, works as a security guard. They have a teenage daughter named Sarah who has serious mental impairments. They are afraid that because of the new financial problems they face, they can no longer afford Sarah's caretaker and will have to send their daughter to a state institution.*
>
> *On Yvonne's second visit to the Carson home, she notices that Sarah has badly bruised legs, and on the third visit she sees that the teenager has wrist burns. When she mentions the discoloration to Alice, the mother reveals that her daughter is sometimes violent and has to be restrained. Alice also tells Yvonne that she believes that the caretaker may be striking Sarah. Alice is afraid that if she fires the helper she won't be able to replace her. Even though the family has financial problems, it is important to them to keep Sarah at home. Without help, Alice would have to quit her job, remain in the home, and try to handle Sarah on her own during the day, which she feels will be more than she can manage.*

Discussion of Ethical Standards

The following are the primary NVASC ethical standards that apply to this sample scenario:

Ethical Standard 1.4: *The victim assistance provider achieves and maintains a high level of professional competence.*

How does professional competence apply in this scenario?

While Yvonne is described as an experienced advocate for victims of financial crime, there is no indication in the description that Yvonne has expertise in child abuse and/or abuse of people with disabilities. The Carsons need assistance from a financial crime advocate and Sarah needs advocacy from an individual experienced in child abuse cases and assisting individuals with mental impairments.

Ethical Standard 3.5: *The victim assistance provider preserves the confidentiality of information provided by the person served or acquired from other sources before, during, and after the course of the professional relationship.*

Does the confidentiality rule apply to Yvonne's conversation with Alice?

As her advocate, Yvonne has a duty to respect the confidentiality of Alice's remarks, but also has the duty to assess the danger posed to Sarah. Yvonne must report the abuse when there is evidence of clear danger from abuse or serious neglect of her needs.

Ethical Standard 3.2: *The victim assistance provider recognizes the interests of the person served as a primary responsibility.*

Who is/are the primary client(s)?

Yvonne was sent to assist the Carsons as victims of financial crime. She learns that Sarah may be a victim of abuse. Yvonne's duty is to seek an ethical and appropriate solution for all members of the family. Furthermore, the caretaker accused of abuse has not had the opportunity to respond to the allegations. Alice could be lying or protecting Joe. Alice may also have angered Joe for acknowledging the abuse to Yvonne and endangered herself. Finally, no one has listened to Joe's point of view about the abuse to Sarah.

Ethical Standard 1.1: *The victim assistance provider understands his or her legal responsibilities, limitations, and the implications of his or her actions within the service delivery setting and performs duties in accord with laws, regulations, policies, and legislated rights of persons served.*

Is Yvonne's duty to report the abuse absolute?

Yvonne requires more information. A sensitive inquiry to assess the degree of abuse to Sarah would be the next step in determining her duty to report.

Ethical Standard 1.3: *The victim assistance provider maintains a high standard of professional conduct.*

What is Yvonne's ethical responsibility to her agency and allied professionals?

A serious error in judgment on Yvonne's part will reflect negatively on her agency. In a complex dilemma of this nature, she should request the advice and support of her colleagues in dealing with the various issues presented. If and when it is appropriate to contact Child Protective Services (CPS) concerning Sarah, Yvonne should strive to be open, professional, and collaborative in her interactions with the outside agency. Again, confidentiality issues should be considered.

More information and an in-depth analysis of the pros and cons of the situation are required for Yvonne to resolve the ethical dilemmas that she faces in her efforts to help Sarah, Alice, and Joe Carson. Assistance from a colleague with expertise in child abuse is also essential. A short version of the ethical decision-making model for analyzing the dilemmas Yvonne faces is described below.

Model for Analyzing Ethical Dilemmas

Application of the model to resolve the ethical dilemmas presented by the Carsons' situation is a three-step process that assesses the case details, separates the practical considerations from the ethical considerations, and projects the potential upsides and downsides of possible courses of action.

Part 1: Assess case details.

Yvonne's primary role is to assist the Carsons in dealing with problems arising from their financial victimization.

Sarah requires an advocate to address abuse issues.

Alice has conveyed to Yvonne that the caretaker strikes Sarah but also admits to physically restraining her when she is not manageable.

Alice expresses a strong desire to keep Sarah at home rather than send her to an institution.

Yvonne needs to engage the support of her colleagues and/or other agencies.

Yvonne is mandated to report abuse.

Part 2: Separate practical considerations from ethical considerations.

PRACTICAL CONSIDERATIONS	ETHICAL CONSIDERATIONS
Yvonne has no experience assisting victims of abuse or victims with disabilities.	1.3 Maintain a high level of professional competency.
Alleged abuse by the caretaker. Abusive treatment of Sarah during attempts to restrain her.	3.5 Confidentiality of information.
As victims of financial crime, the Carsons need assistance from Yvonne.	3.2 Primary responsibility is the interests of the person(s) served.
Legal obligation on suspected abuse. Agency policy.	1.1 Understand legal responsibilities.
Yvonne represents her agency.	1.3 Professional conduct.

Part 3: What are the potential upsides of the following courses of action? What are the potential downsides?

OPTION 1: Yvonne maintains Alice's confidence, does not report the abuse, and identifies a community-based child advocate for the Carsons to contact as a condition of nonreporting.

Positive Outcome. Yvonne focuses her efforts on the Carsons' financial victimization. Alice and Joe engage the support of the advocate experienced in child abuse and mental impairment who helps them identify the source of the abuse and assess the degree of harm caused to Sarah. Yvonne will have found a means to address the abuse, respected Alice's right to confidentiality, and avoided a lengthy investigation by Child Protective Services that would be a difficult and potentially embarrassing experience for the Carsons.

Negative Outcome. The intervention on the child abuse is unsuccessful. The caretaker quits rather than take the blame for the abuse and Alice is left to care for Sarah. Alice does not come to terms with the fact that her way of restraining Sarah when she is upset is also abusive. Joe refuses to work with the child advocate, saying it does not concern him as he is not the abuser. Yvonne's failure to report the abuse will be perceived as an error in ethical duty that may harm the credibility of her agency. The child abuse advocate files a report with Child Protective Services.

Option 2: Yvonne maintains Alice's confidence, the Carsons fire the caretaker, and Alice agrees to stay at home with Sarah with the understanding that both she and Joe will take classes in caring for children with mental impairments and undergo counseling to deal with the abuse problems.

Positive Outcome. The family system stays intact. Alice and Joe commit to learning how to take better care of Sarah. They also work out their financial problems as a result of the credit-card scam so that Joe can cut back on his hours at work and share responsibility for Sarah.

Negative Outcome. If the counseling experience is unsuccessful, the old patterns could be perpetuated. Joe becomes bored staying at home during the day and leaves the responsibility for caring for Sarah with Alice. She becomes angry and frustrated by her lack of freedom and Sarah's difficult behavior. Yvonne finds herself informally monitoring the family long after the financial problems are solved and eventually calls for an intervention from Child Protective Services.

Option 3: Yvonne reports the suspected abuse to Child Protective Services (CPS).

Positive Outcome. Sarah's abuse is professionally assessed and sensitively addressed; she receives support and advocacy; and arrangements for better outside care are made. Yvonne focuses on the financial victimization and fulfills her legal duty to report abuse. Her obligation to correctly represent the ethical standards of her agency is met.

Negative Outcome. The family environment deteriorates as a result of the CPS intervention. Alice and Joe both resent the invasion of privacy. Alice feels shame and humiliation over the outside intervention; she loses faith in Yvonne and the helping process, and rejects her advocacy. Joe blames Alice for revealing the abuse information to Yvonne in the first place. Sarah receives better professional care but her parents are always angry.

Alice and Joe's situation *is* complex. Yvonne has a great many variables that she must consider in deciding what her role should be in assisting the Carsons, maintaining her ethical standards, and arriving at the best possible result for the family.

In the field of victim assistance, providers can count on the fact that they will regularly deal with the results of people's inability to negotiate the complexities of their lives. The situations are rarely black and white and resolving them often requires consideration of several factors and opposing points of view. In chapter 5, a short version of this ethical decision-making model is presented for use in the analysis of sample ethical dilemmas based on the NVASC Ethical Standards. Readers have the opportunity to analyze each dilemma, identify the practical considerations, review the relevant standards, and reflect on actions and outcomes.

Conclusion

When ethical codes come into conflict in a provider's service to a client or among intra-agency service providers or allied professionals, there may be many ways to resolve the dilemma. Thoughtful analysis and reflection, cultivation of open communication in adversarial situations, and a workplace environment in which consultation with colleagues feels safe and is productive will be the best way to solve the dilemma. Providers who develop the ability to analyze ethical dilemmas from all perspectives, who can determine the victim assistance ethical codes that apply in a particular dilemma, and who review all options with an open mind will navigate the resolution process more effectively.

References

Evans, Kit. 1980. "A Feminist Perspective on the Ethics of Communication." Appended and expanded in 1998 by Lisa Olcese and Lisa Calderon. Boulder, Colo.: Safehouse Progressive Alliance for Nonviolence, Inc.
Weston, A. 1997. *A Practical Companion to Ethics*. New York: Oxford University Press.

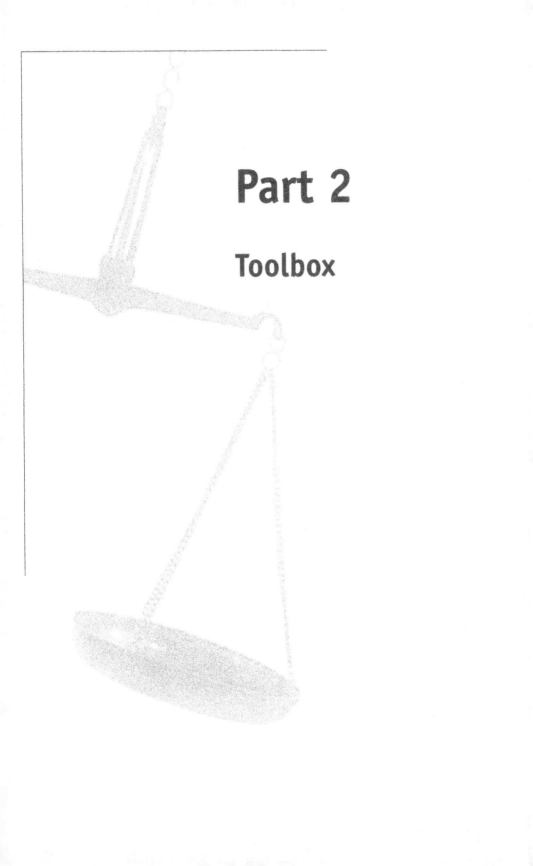

Part 2

Toolbox

CHAPTER 5

Applying Ethical Standards in the Real World

This chapter focuses on the application of the NVASC Ethical Standards to possible scenarios involving the delivery of victim services. Since the field of victim services is, by nature, multidisciplinary, these scenarios involve a great diversity of situations, providers, and possible outcomes. As has been discussed throughout this text, arriving at an appropriate course of action and/or behavior is largely a process of deciding how best to identify, meet the needs, and serve the interests of all parties involved while respecting the ethical standards of the profession. Developing a win-win solution to these situations may not be easy. Situations will arise, sometimes on a daily basis, for which there are no easy or established answers. Naturally, many scenarios are illustrative of more than one ethical standard simultaneously.

The following scenarios are a compilation of stories and experiences submitted by victim assistance providers from across the nation who were interviewed about ethical issues they deal with on a regular basis. Some of the scenarios have been modified to better fit the intention of the standard or to add complexity to the analytical process of ethical decision-making. Every effort has been made to create scenarios that are realistic, relevant, and respectful of the challenges that victim assistance providers from all disciplines commonly face.

The scenarios underwent a peer review process several times during the development of the text. Not surprisingly, service providers' interpretations of specific dilemmas varied considerably in each review. Their responses confirmed the assumption that approaches to ethical decision-making are directly related to the philosophical orientation of the provider organization or agency and the nature of the service provided. Peer reviewers interpreted the ethical dilemmas in these scenarios based on their experience and training in the workplace.

There was also a prioritization of importance of ethical standards in each scenario as part of the peer review process that varied among providers according to their job descriptions. In other words, community-based rape crisis advocates who peer-reviewed the scenarios focused on different aspects of ethical dilemmas than did victim witness advocates from district attorneys' offices.

The scenarios have been designed for use by individual readers to think through ethical decision-making processes that involve ethical standards in combination and in a variety of contexts. The scenarios also lend themselves to role-play in training environments; they allow opportunities for disagreement over proposed outcomes; and they set up a rich environment for cross training among victim assistance system- and community-based organizations.

Each ethical standard is presented with a scenario in accordance with the four main categories created by the Consortium:

- Scope of services
- Coordinating with the community
- Direct services
- Administration and evaluation

Following each proposed ethical standard is the sample scenario that presents one or more ethical dilemmas that illustrate the intention of the code. The Ethical Decision-Making Model presented in chapter 4 is applied in this chapter to analyze each scenario:

- The details of the case are assessed.
- The factors that contribute to the ethical dilemma(s) are identified.
- The practical considerations of the scenario are separated from the ethical considerations.
- Two possible responses are presented.
- Possible positive and negative outcomes are briefly discussed.

Scope of Services

Ethical Standard 1.1: Victim assistance providers must understand their legal responsibilities, limitations, and the implications of their actions within the service delivery setting. They must perform their duties in accordance with the existing laws, regulations, policies, and legislated rights of the people they serve.

Sue is a sexual assault victim assistance provider who has been called to the emergency room to assist a victim. When she arrives, she finds Connie, the victim, in a room with a police officer. Connie, who has a hearing impairment, is too embarrassed to describe the intimate details of the rape with the police officer present. At times, her speech is difficult to understand. Eventually, the officer agrees to leave the room, but asks Sue to report the details to him after she hears Connie's story. In accordance with her agency's policy, Sue declines because she realizes that doing as the officer asks would put her confidential relationship with Connie at risk, allowing her to be subpoenaed if the case comes to trial. As an alternative, and because no sexual assault nurse examiner is present, Sue suggests the emergency room doctor take the information from Connie. However, the ER doctor has a clinical manner and is impatient when Connie does not speak clearly. Connie becomes extremely upset.

Service providers *must* know all the statutes that govern all aspects of victims' rights and services in their state and they must act within the scope of those statutes. A victim assistance provider who has an insufficient knowledge of the specifics of the legal authority under which he or she works may unintentionally follow unethical practices, violate the law, and/or cause harm to the victim.

Part 1: Assess case details.

Sue's goals are to:

support Connie in this period of crisis;

help Connie understand her rights and the services that are available to her;

identify Connie's needs so she can work to meet them;

preserve the confidentiality of information Connie discloses to her; and

find a way to communicate clearly with Connie despite her hearing impairment.

Part 2: Separate practical considerations from ethical considerations.

PRACTICAL CONSIDERATIONS	ETHICAL CONSIDERATIONS
Agency policy/state laws.	1.1 Understand legal responsibilities.
Sue's need to know how to help Connie. Lack of legal protection from subpoena.	3.5 Confidentiality of information.
Fragile emotional state of victim.	3.2 Primary responsibility is the interests of person served.

Part 3: What are the potential upsides of the following courses of action? What are the potential downsides?

OPTION 1: Sue speaks to Connie in private about her needs and concerns, and explains to her what will happen during the examination. Sue lets Connie know that she does not need to know the details of the crime because she may not be able to keep the information confidential.

Positive Outcome: Connie is calmer and able to communicate more clearly with Sue. She agrees to the rape kit examination. The officer agrees to conduct the interview with Connie the following day at the police station when Connie might feel less vulnerable and traumatized.

Negative Outcome: Sue inadvertently learns personal details from Connie that might negatively influence the outcome of the case. These details come out later and Connie reveals that Sue was party to the information. Sue is subpoenaed, and accused of suppressing evidence, creating an embarrassing situation for her agency.

OPTION 2: Sue locates a female counselor in the hospital who knows American Sign Language and is therefore better able to communicate with Connie. Sue asks the counselor to speak with Connie and help facilitate the interview between Connie and the police officer.

Positive Outcome: With the help of the interpreter, Sue explains Connie's rights and the services available to her. After speaking with the police officer, Connie seeks services with the rape crisis center and support during the criminal justice process.

Negative Outcome: The deaf and hearing-impaired community is small and Connie knows of the counselor who communicates with American Sign Language at the hospital. She prefers not to reveal any details of the rape to her lest her hearing-impaired friends find out what happened to her.

These are only a few of the possible outcomes that might result from actions that Sue takes in her efforts to assist Connie in the aftermath of the rape. In the next four sample scenarios, readers are presented with options for solving the ethical dilemma. Take some time to consider the potential positive and negative implications of each option. Remember, these outcomes are not presented as "right" or "wrong" answers. Rather they are possible plausible results of the particular courses of action suggested.

Ethical Standard 1.2: *Victim assistance providers must accurately represent their professional title, qualifications, and/or credentials in relationships with their clients and in public advertising.*

Everyone at the community-based domestic violence center loves Chantal. She has been a volunteer hotline counselor for ten years. As a domestic violence survivor herself, Chantal feels that she is well equipped to listen to victims and support them as they try to rebuild their lives. When victims call in for legal advice, as one option she offers to set up an appointment with the legal advocate who provides referrals to pro bono lawyers. For several months, however, Chantal has been presenting legal options over the telephone with regard to protection orders and custody because she feels that she understands the issues. Two different victims mention to their advocates that Chantal "got it right" when it came to talking to the family court judge. A few weeks later, however, a victim complains that Chantal gave her terrible legal advice and that she shouldn't be answering calls from people in crisis.

Crime victims assume that the information that providers offer them is reliable and accurate. Providers should not misrepresent their advocacy or professional abilities in service to the victim or in their responsibilities to the organization and their colleagues.

Part 1: Assess case details.

> Chantal is seriously committed to assisting crime victims as a volunteer hotline counselor.
>
> Chantal is violating organization guidelines by giving advice rather than presenting options. She is also breaking the law through unauthorized practice of law.
>
> Protocol requires that volunteers refer victims with legal questions to the staff advocates.
>
> Staff members had been aware that Chantal was out of line, but they overlooked it until there was a negative outcome.

Part 2: Separate practical considerations from ethical considerations.

PRACTICAL CONSIDERATIONS	ETHICAL CONSIDERATIONS
Chantal's ten years of experience as a peer hotline counselor.	1.2 Accurate representation of credentials.
Rules about unauthorized practice of law.	1.1 Understand legal responsibilities.
Endangering the well-being and reputation of an agency.	1.3 Respect for relationships with colleagues and other professionals.
Staff failed to intervene when they learned that Chantal was giving legal advice.	4.1 Report the conduct of colleagues if it brings the profession into dishonor.

Part 3: What are the potential upsides of the following courses of action? What are the potential downsides?

Option 1: The center chooses to be discreet in their handling of the matter. The volunteer supervisor asks Chantal to come by the office to meet with the legal advocates to discuss hotline protocols.

Positive Outcome: Chantal did not know that unauthorized practice of law is illegal and could result in a lawsuit against the center. She expresses remorse and promises to stop talking about legal matters with the clients. After the meeting, Chantal develops language to use whenever the clients ask her legal advice so that she can direct inquiries to the staff.

Negative Outcome: Chantal stops talking about legal matters but she does not restrict herself from talking about her own experiences of domestic violence with the hotline callers. It turns out that Chantal has never had training on boundary issues and that very few guidelines on ethics have ever been provided to the volunteers.

OPTION 2: The volunteer supervisor decides to conduct an informal survey among the hotline volunteers to determine the kinds of conversations they are having with clients without revealing there has been a problem. She discovers that several lack training on ethical issues. She schedules in-service sessions for the volunteer staff to experience a refresher course on hotline protocols and ethical practices.

Positive Outcome: The volunteer staff understands why they have protocols and policies in place that guide them in their hotline conversations with domestic violence victims. They receive an in-depth training in the ethical issues that come up regularly in the service of victims.

Negative Outcome: When a victim goes to the newspaper and reports that the center allows the volunteers to give legal advice, the center comes under attack. Not talking about Chantal's mistakes and not addressing the group as a whole to discuss the mistake leaves doubts in many of the volunteers' minds of their appropriate roles. Several quit and the hotline remains short-staffed for months.

Ethical Standard 1.3: *Victim assistance providers must maintain a high standard of professional conduct.*

Joe has recently been hired as the victim liaison for a local community corrections department. He loves golf but can only afford to play at the public golf course. One weekend, while waiting for his wife at a favorite spot in town, he meets George, a man whose son has recently been released on probation after a DUI that involved a serious injury. Joe has received information from the victim's family that the youth is not respecting his conditions of release. At one point in the conversation, Joe admits to George that he is aware of problems in his son's case because he works in the supervisory agency as the victim liaison. As Joe leaves, George hands him a business card and three guest passes to a private golf club. George also tells Joe that if his son gives him any trouble, he should give him a call because he knows how to keep the boy in line. Joe smiles gratefully, and promises to keep George advised. He also thanks George for his generosity, but, as George leaves, Joe realizes he has behaved improperly.

Providers must not only avoid improper behavior, but avoid even the *appearance* of impropriety. In maintaining a high degree of professional conduct, providers must not use their positions to obtain special favors, privileges, advantages, gifts, or access to services that are unrelated to agency interests or that serve them personally.

Part 1: Assess case details.

Agency policy prevents Joe from sharing confidential information with an outsider about any case.

Joe has accepted a favor with the promise of a return of favor that he cannot ethically fulfill.

Joe's behavior is inappropriate and unprofessional for a representative of a criminal justice agency.

Joe is entering into a dual relationship.

Part 2: Separate practical considerations from ethical considerations.

PRACTICAL CONSIDERATIONS	ETHICAL CONSIDERATIONS
Accepting favors.	1.3 Professional conduct.
Harm to the victim.	3.5 Confidentiality of information.
Agency policy/state laws.	3.2 Primary responsibility is the interests of person served.
Self-interest and overstating the freedom he has to reveal information.	3.6 Conflict of interest.

Part 3: What are the potential upsides of the following courses of action? What are the downsides?

OPTION 1: Joe realizes he has engaged in improper behavior for a victim assistance provider and reports his conduct to his superiors. Joe writes George a note of apology, copies his superior, and returns the passes.

Positive Outcome. Self-reporting lessens the potential for harm to the victim or the agency and helps Joe remember the boundaries he must maintain between his social life and his professional life.

Negative Outcome. Joe has lost an opportunity to establish a professionally appropriate rapport with George as the father of a difficult and potentially dangerous offender, which might have served the interests of the victim and of the community.

OPTION 2: Joe informs his boss that he has information from the victim's family that the DUI offender is not respecting his conditions of release, and suggests bringing George, the young man's father, on board (without revealing the victim's complaint) to help monitor the situation. He does not mention the golf passes.

Positive Outcome: Joe establishes a professionally appropriate rapport with George as the father of a difficult and potentially dangerous offender, which can serve the interests of the victim and of the community.

Negative Outcome: Joe's relationship with his superiors and his relationship with George continue to be compromised by his lack of disclosure and his acceptance of favors.

Ethical Standard 1.4: *Victim assistance providers must achieve and maintain a high level of professional competence.*

June, who is Caucasian, switched careers at midlife. She went from having her own psychotherapy practice in a small midwestern town to being the victim services coordinator for a large metropolitan police department. For the past ten years, she has supervised the work of several victim assistance providers in her department and offered advocacy services directly to victims. June is particularly fond of Mehina, an angry young Sudanese immigrant who came in to file a report on her boyfriend after he threatened to kidnap her young daughter. Over the course of a few meetings, June realizes that Mehina has severe mental health problems exacerbated by harsh parents and a traditional upbringing, and that these issues contribute to the volatile situation in which she now lives. Because of her history as a psychotherapist, June decides Mehina needs therapy in order to see more clearly the patterns in her life, deal with her anger issues, and understand the threat these issues pose for her daughter. In her previous career, however, she has no experience working with people of Mehina's culture. June also believes Mehina will not seek the help she needs on her own.

In serving the best needs of the victim, providers must stay within the clearly defined range of their roles and responsibilities. If the victims' needs go beyond these particular skills, providers must make an outside referral. To do this, providers must be familiar with the resources of the communities in which they work and have contacts within the allied professionals in the area.

Part 1: Assess case details.

The provision of psychological services is beyond the scope of June's job description at the police department.

June is not culturally competent to effectively help Mehina with her family problems.

June is considering an informal change to the nature of the victim-client relation without permission from the client.

The safety of Mehina's daughter should be dealt with as soon as possible.

Part 2: Separate practical considerations from ethical considerations.

PRACTICAL CONSIDERATIONS	ETHICAL CONSIDERATIONS
June's inexperience working with multicultural clients in a therapeutic context.	1.4 Professional competence.
June's job description as an administrator.	1.3 Professional conduct.
Safety concerns for Mehina's daughter.	1.1 Understand legal responsibilities.
Mehina's anger issues.	3.2 Primary responsibility is the interest of the person served.

Part 3: What are the potential upsides of the following courses? What are the potential downsides?

Option 1: June expresses her concerns to Mehina about her anger issues and her daughter's well-being, lets Mehina know of her prior career, and explains that she is unable to fulfill that role in her present position but will identify an appropriate mental-health referral.

Positive Outcome: June suggests a professionally and culturally competent mental-health professional who could conduct evaluations of both Mehina and her daughter. Mehina agrees to be evaluated and leaves with the referral.

Negative Outcome: Mehina decides that the violence in the family is all her fault and does not return to the law enforcement agency. June does not have any feedback as to her progress and remains uninformed about the daughter's safety. Mehina changes homes and begins to slip through the cracks.

Option 2: June discusses Mehina's family issues with her and asks permission to evaluate Mehina's daughter. Her lack of understanding of Sudanese culture curtails her ability to be helpful. Soon after, Mehina's daughter is placed in a dangerous situation that is reported and the child is put in the care of Child Protective Services.

Positive Outcome: When her daughter goes into foster care Mehina realizes that she should seriously address her own problems if she wants to raise her own child. She takes steps to do so. Her child is soon returned to her and she ends all contact with her boyfriend.

Negative Outcome: Mehina is angry with June and angry with everyone in the system for taking her daughter away. June understands her anger issues and offers to intervene on her behalf, but Mehina no longer trusts her. The boyfriend continues to be a negative factor in the family dynamic.

Ethical Standard 1.5: *Victim assistance providers who provide a service for a fee must inform the client of the fee at the initial session.*

Ellen is a counselor at a rape crisis center with more clients than she can handle. She has been working with a particularly vulnerable college student named Sheila for over a year. Sheila often fails to show up at appointments.

Ellen decides to move her into a weekly fee-based group counseling session that meets in the evening to make room in her schedule for clients with more immediate needs. It takes a lot of time and coaxing to convince Sheila that the move to a group and another counselor will be beneficial, so much so that Ellen forgets to mention the $5.00 charge per session. At the end of the first group session when the other women hand over their payments, Sheila bursts into tears because she has no money to pay for the session. Sheila complains to the new counselor that Ellen first abandoned her and has now humiliated her.

Full and accurate information concerning when payment is expected, whether insurance may cover any expenses, how payment is handled, and the policy regarding missed or canceled appointments must be clearly communicated before services are delivered.

Part 1: Assess case details.

Sheila was accustomed to free and private counseling services.

Sheila's participation in scheduled sessions is not reliable.

Ellen is overworked.

Ellen forgot to tell Sheila about the $5.00 charge.

Sheila feels that Ellen abandoned her.

Trust issues develop between the victim assistance provider and the victim.

Part 2: Separate practical considerations from ethical considerations.

PRACTICAL CONSIDERATIONS	ETHICAL CONSIDERATIONS
Ability-to-pay considerations.	1.5 Advanced notice of fee for services.
Ellen is overworked; compassion fatigue.	1.4 Professional competence.
Sheila needs help but fails to show up for her private appointments, showing a lack of respect for Ellen.	3.2 Primary responsibility is the interest of the person served.
A counseling relationship gone "stale."	3.7 Termination of a professional relationship.

Part 3: What are the potential upsides of the following courses of action? What are the potential downsides?

OPTION 1: Ellen apologizes to Sheila for forgetting to mention the fee. Ellen attends the evening counseling sessions for a few weeks to ease Sheila into the group activity. She leaves the door open for Shelia to return to private counseling.

Positive Outcome: Sheila joins the group and finds that she enjoys the change.

Negative Outcome: Ellen is unable to address her own stress and burnout and continues to put energy into her relationship with Sheila when it would be better for another advocate to take on Sheila as a client if she needs to be in private counseling.

OPTION 2: Ellen feels defensive when Sheila puts her on the spot about the fee. She decides that she has reached a point where she can no longer be helpful to Sheila and turns the situation over to her supervisor to handle. Ellen asks for a few medical days off so that she can relax and reassess her work situation.

Positive Outcome: Ellen lets go of a counseling relationship that has no longer appears to be beneficial to the client and begins to address her burnout.

Negative Outcome: The manner in which Ellen deals with Sheila is perceived of as negative and Sheila feels rejected.

Coordinating with the Community

Ethical Standard 2.1: Victim assistance providers must conduct their relationships with colleagues and other professionals in such a way as to promote mutual respect, public confidence, and improvement of service.

David is the chief district attorney and is being honored at a political dinner given by the county bar association for his public service work. He is well liked and popular among his constituents and is known for his get-tough policy on crime. However, the local domestic violent coalition is locking horns with him over the way he has interpreted the no-drop policy, which the coalition originally promoted. A batterer in the community has recently carried out his threat to murder his wife if she ever brought charges against him, threats that were communicated to everyone from the prosecutor to the police to the victim's pastor at church. After David's thank-you speech, Emma, a victim assistance provider at the shelter, realizes she will have the opportunity to stand up and ask him publicly to defend his no-drop policy.

It is important for victim assistance providers to contribute, whenever and wherever possible, to public confidence and respect for their agency and the field. When making statements in a public context, providers should clarify if they are speaking on their own behalf, as a representative of their agency, or on behalf of all victim assistance providers.

Part 1: Assess case details.

Goal is to draw attention to how the no-drop policy was administered.

Potentially effective (but perhaps poor) choice of venue.

Potential success or failure of delivery of message.

Potential embarrassment caused to a district attorney and an agency that victim service providers rely on for victims' rights implementation and collaboration.

Potential harm caused to Emma's organization.

Lack of permission from her boss (who is on vacation) to speak on behalf of the agency.

Part 2: Separate practical considerations from ethical considerations.

PRACTICAL CONSIDERATIONS	ETHICAL CONSIDERATIONS
The DA ignores the opinion of local domestic violence advocates and remains poorly informed about domestic violence issues.	2.1 Respect for relationships with colleagues and other professionals.

PRACTICAL CONSIDERATIONS	ETHICAL CONSIDERATIONS
The implementation of the local no-drop policy has had a lethal outcome for a domestic violence victim.	3.2 Primary responsibility is the interests of person(s) served.
Finding opportunities to be heard in a public venue.	2.3 Contribute to the improvement of systems that impact victims.

Part 3: What are the potential upsides of the following courses of action? What are the potential downsides?

OPTION 1: Emma plans ahead by briefing a news reporter on the telephone about the no-drop policy and invites him to accompany her when she questions the DA at the reception before the dinner. The encounter with the DA is cordial but inconclusive. Two days later an article appears in the newspaper on domestic violence in the county that discusses the no-drop policy and quotes the DA in the context of the recent homicide. The DA considers a reevaluation of the policy.

Positive Outcome: The policy is reevaluated and no harm is caused to the interagency relationship. The public has an opportunity to be educated about domestic violence issues in the county.

Negative Outcome: Emma misses an opportunity to put the intense pressure that may be necessary on the prosecutor to learn more about domestic violence and to change policy.

OPTION 2: Emma speaks out aggressively on the no-drop policy at the dinner, but is quickly asked to sit down by a member of the bar association. A chaotic and loud argument ensues involving several members of the audience. The local reporter captures the scene in a front-page article the next day but is critical of Emma's behavior and the organization that she represents.

Positive Outcome: Emma has called attention to the issue of the no-drop policy with the DA. The media calls for a formal evaluation of the policy. The evaluation prompts modifications to the no-drop policy that demonstrate greater sensitivity to the concerns of battered women.

Negative Outcome: The DA is angry at Emma and her organization. The next time an important issue arises between the two offices, the DA ignores the domestic violence center's input. Opportunities for cross-training and collaboration between the two offices diminish. Emma's boss returns from vacation and is angry with her for acting in a way that is harmful to the organization.

These are only two of the possible outcomes from actions Emma might take in her efforts to change the no-drop policy within the prosecutor's office and prompt them to increase their knowledge of domestic violence issues.

In the next two sample scenarios, providers are presented with options for solving the ethical dilemma. Take some time to consider the potential positive and negative implications of each option. Remember, these outcomes are not presented as "right" or "wrong" answers. Rather they are possible plausible results of the particular courses of action suggested.

 Ethical Standard 2.2: *Victim assistance providers must share their knowledge with their colleagues and encourage proficiency among their colleagues and other professionals.*

Diane and Sam recently attended a restorative justice conference where they learned how to conduct a healing circle for victims. Upon their return, they excitedly approached their boss, Peg, at the probation office, and asked if they could bring someone in to conduct an in-service training for the victim assistance personnel. Peg had already assigned the rest of her training budget to a program for five new volunteers on how to talk to and assist victims, but she asked her supervisor for permission. He was skeptical. "I don't want any of that touchy-feely stuff happening in my office," he replied. "If you want to spend your limited training budget on this activity, that's fine. But don't come to me for more money later when you want to train new volunteers."

Victim assistance providers must be ready and encouraged to share their knowledge, expertise, and skills with other practitioners both in and out of the workplace, including both paid and volunteer workers. Volunteers have access to the information, training, and resources they need to do their jobs properly and effectively.

Part 1: Assess case details.

Peg would like to see restorative justice practices integrated into the agency.

Diane and Sam are anxious to share important new knowledge.

The supervisor assigns Peg an insufficient budget for training and in-service activities.

The supervisor is dismissive of restorative justice principles and does not appear to understand them.

There is a shortage of adequately trained volunteers on hand to assist victims.

Part 2: Separate practical considerations from ethical considerations.

PRACTICAL CONSIDERATIONS	ETHICAL CONSIDERATIONS
Validation of Diane and Sam's newly acquired knowledge and desire to share it with colleagues.	2.2 Sharing knowledge with colleagues and encouraging proficiency.
Need for a harmonious relationship with the supervisor.	2.1 Respect for relationships with colleagues and other professionals.
Need for more volunteers with basic competency skills working with victims.	2.3 Contribute to the improvement of systems that impact victims.

Part 3: What are the potential upsides of the following courses of action? What are the potential downsides?

Option 1: Peg develops a twelve-month in-service plan for training volunteers and staff that sets goals, establishes priorities, and creates a timetable both for training volunteers and introducing restorative justice practices into the agency. Without mentioning healing circles, she presents the program to the supervisor and asks him sign off on the budget. He agrees.

Positive Outcome: Several months later, as part of the restorative justice programming, Peg allows Diane and Sam to bring in a trainer to conduct a healing circle. The two advocates are thrilled to see their idea come to fruition and the training is well attended.

Negative Outcome: The supervisor is irritated when he realizes that Peg "hid" the costs of the healing circle in the budget and managed to do volunteer training as well. After that, whenever she needs funds for restorative justice programming, the supervisor always denies her request.

OPTION 2: Peg reports back to Diane and Sam that the supervisor will only authorize training on healing circles at the expense of volunteer training. They will have to wait for another opportunity to apply for funds, or conduct the training themselves on a weekend on staff free time. She promises to give them continuing education credits.

Positive Outcome: This situation places the responsibility on Diane and Sam to conduct the training on the staff's free time. It validates their desire to share the new skills they have acquired. If they agree, Peg gets to introduce restorative justice principles into the agency without interference from the supervisor.

Negative Outcome: There is no change to the supervisor's attitude about restorative justice because he has no exposure to it. The staff members at the agency are overworked as it is and they shouldn't have to train on weekends just because the head of the agency is shortsighted about important emerging programs.

Ethical Standard 2.3: *Victim assistance providers serve the public interest by contributing to the improvement of systems that impact victims of crime.*

Marian is the new director of an understaffed county domestic violence center where heavy workloads are a growing problem. Part of the center's community outreach program during National Domestic Violence Awareness Month is to maintain a booth at the local mall on the weekends so they can meet with the public and answer questions. But when it comes down to signing up for a four-hour session and staffing the booth, half the employees claim to have important responsibilities in their private lives that prevent their participation. The result is that every year the same people get stuck with mall duty, and they have begun to resent it. Still others feel they are not paid enough to give up their weekends even though they are compensated for the time they will spend conducting outreach. Marian feels it is important that everyone participates but is uncomfortable in her role as "enforcer."

Providers take part in professional or community activities that educate the public about victims' rights, victims' concerns and availability of services.

Part 1: Assess case details.

The domestic violence center is understaffed and overworked.

The center has the responsibility to reach out to the public and make them aware of the available services.

The staff within the center should receive equal and fair treatment.

Marian is unsure in her role as a leader.

Part 2: Separate practical considerations from ethical considerations.

PRACTICAL CONSIDERATIONS	ETHICAL CONSIDERATIONS
Mandate to improve public education about victims' rights and services.	2.3 Contribute to the improvement of systems that impact victims.
Resentment over lack of fair play.	2.1 Respect for relationships with colleagues and other professionals.
Unhappy, underpaid, and overworked staff; risk of burnout.	1.4 Professional competence.

Part 3: What are the potential upsides of the following courses of action? What are the potential downsides?

OPTION 1: Marian holds a staff meeting and informs them that it is her opinion that staff members who fail to participate in the outreach program are violating an ethical standard. She asks the entire staff to vote on one of two remedies: institute repercussions for nonattending staff or reward attending staff with compensatory time during other times of the year equal to the hours spent staffing the booth.

Positive Outcome: The staff chooses to reward those who attend on weekends at the mall with free days. Marian dodges the "enforcer" role and achieves staff buy-in by making them be responsible for deciding how they will handle the lack of participation. Those people who want to work harder do so and feel that they are treated fairly.

Negative Outcome: The people that are willing to work weekends at the mall are suffering from burnout and need their weekends to recuperate.

Option 2: Marian concedes that working in the booth at the mall on weekends may be too much to ask, and requests that the volunteer coordinator recruit and train volunteers to conduct the public outreach at the mall.

Positive Outcome: The problem with unfair treatment among the staff disappears. Marian has more time to focus on staff members who are potentially suffering from burnout.

Negative Outcome: There are questions that volunteers can't answer or answer incorrectly and sometimes the agency has to correct information volunteers have given to the public, causing everyone considerable frustration.

Direct Services

Ethical Standard 3.1: *Victim assistance providers must respect and attempt to protect the victim's civil rights.*

Jhala appears with her two young daughters at the hospital emergency room with serious head injuries following a domestic dispute. She is a recent Muslim immigrant from the Middle East. Jhala is adamantly refusing to be examined by a male emergency room doctor when Charmaine, an African American victim assistance provider, intervenes on her behalf. Charmaine's brother is a member of the Nation of Islam and she is familiar with the cultural mores that discourage Muslim women from being alone with males who are not their family members. Arrangements are made for Jhala to see a female doctor, who then requests that Jhala have x-rays to check for a concussion. The x-ray technician is male and, once again, Jhala refuses the service and decides to go home. Before Jhala leaves, Charmaine notices both daughters have badly bruised legs, as if they had been beaten with a belt. Concerned that if she questions Jhala about the girls' bruises, she may become frightened and leave the premises, Charmaine instead asks Jhala if she and the girls would like to spend the night in the domestic violence shelter and return to the hospital in the morning when a female x-ray technician is available. At first, Jhala is afraid to commit what will be considered an act of serious disobedience to her family. However, when Charmaine promises her no one will find out where she is, Jhala eventually agrees.

Part 1: Assess case details.

The details of the victimization thus far are unknown but concerns for the immediate safety of Jhala and her daughters are foremost.

There are likely three victims rather than one victim.

Jhala's concerns as a Muslim woman in a traditional marriage may be beyond the limits of Charmaine's cultural competency.

Charmaine must clearly explain Jhala's rights to her, including the limitations on confidentiality.

The discussion of the girls' bruises on their legs may frighten Jhala away.

Part 2: Separate practical considerations from ethical considerations.

PRACTICAL CONSIDERATIONS	ETHICAL CONSIDERATIONS
Questions over child abuse and an explanation of the limits to confidentiality. Mandated reporting.	3.1 Protect victim's civil rights.
Safety issues, fear, and injuries to the daughters.	3.2 Primary responsibility is the interests of person(s) served.

PRACTICAL CONSIDERATIONS	ETHICAL CONSIDERATIONS
Suggestion that Jhala stay in the shelter, which will be considered an act of disobedience by her family.	3.4 Right to self-determination.
Jhala's religious and cultural values.	1.4 Professional competence.

Part 3: What are the potential upsides of the following courses of action? What are the potential downsides?

OPTION 1: Charmaine explains to Jhala her rights and the services that the domestic violence center offers her, including confidentiality and its limitations. She does not refer specifically to the girls' injuries but lets Jhala know that if it appears that the children are also being victimized, then she will have to bring in Child Protective Services to evaluate the domestic situation.

Positive Outcome: Jhala understands her rights and agrees to go into counseling.

Negative Outcome: During Jhala's x-ray session the following morning, the child abuse advocate at the center speaks with the daughters and learns that they have been whipped as a punishment by their older brother who does not live at home. Jhala is angry that the advocate has spoken to her daughters behind her back, replying that if she had asked her she would have told them the truth. Trust in the professional relationship becomes an issue. Jhala questions whether the center can actually help her solve her problems.

OPTION 2: Charmaine decides that addressing the overall family safety issue is the first priority and concentrates on working with Jhala to establish a safe living environment. She enlists the help of a female Muslim therapist to collaborate on developing an appropriate strategy and safety plan with Jhala. The girls appear to be fine and discussion of the child abuse issue is postponed.

Positive Outcome: Jhala makes substantial progress in coming to terms with her husband's violent behavior. He moves out of the house temporarily and agrees to go into treatment for batterers.

Negative Outcome: The older brother is furious that Jhala has broken up the family and has shown disrespect for his father. He expresses this anger by physically abusing his two little sisters.

These are only two of the possible outcomes that could result from actions that Charmaine might take in her efforts to help Jhala create a safe living situation for herself and her daughters. In the next nine sample scenarios, providers are presented with options for solving the ethical dilemma. Take some time to consider the potential positive and negative implications of each option. Remember, these outcomes are not presented as "right" or "wrong" answers. Rather they are possible plausible results of the particular courses of action suggested.

Ethical Standard 3.2: *Victim assistance providers recognize the interests of the person served as their primary responsibility.*

Lee Chan works at a not-for-profit advocacy center where she provides support to victims of abuse and neglect. Her newest case, Lisa Yueng, is posing a challenge. Lisa is a nineteen-year-old immigrant who lives with her father, sisters, and two aunts and uncles in a Southeast Asian neighborhood of Los Angeles. They suffered greatly in their country of origin, and Lisa feels it is her duty as the oldest daughter to keep her family together in America at all costs. Yet one of Lisa's uncles molests her and Lisa knows that he is harming her. She has lost her appetite and is rapidly losing weight. A nutrition counselor at the community center referred Lisa to Lee Chan. Lee would like Lisa to reveal who is harming her but, like the rest of her family, her uncle has no green card, and Lisa is terrified that an official report of this crime will trigger his deportation, which would make the whole family turn against her. Lee Chan wants to be supportive so she does not encourage Lisa to report the molestation but does convince her to enter therapy. Lee Chan continues to meets with Lisa on a regular basis.

A victim's desires and wants with respect to her situation may contradict options offered by the victim assistance provider. A provider may deeply disagree with a victim's proposed course of action, or nonaction, but the only ethical response is to provide as much information as possible so that the victim can make a fully informed choice.

Part 1: Assess case details.

The dynamics of immigrant families are complex.

Lisa places the well-being of her family over her own safety.

Lee's goal is to prevent further harm to Lisa and possibly others and to take steps to help Lisa address the trauma she has experienced.

Legal factors regarding immigration may protect Lisa but could cause the deportation of her uncle.

Options are available to stop the abuse without identifying the perpetrator.

Part 2: Separate practical considerations from ethical considerations.

PRACTICAL CONSIDERATIONS	ETHICAL CONSIDERATIONS
Lee Chan's desire for justice and safety for Lisa.	3.2 Primary responsibility is the interest of the person served.
Nondisclosure of the uncle's criminal behavior.	3.4 Right to self-determination.
Southeast Asian family values in conflict with American attitudes about family violence.	1.4 Professional competence.

Part 3: What are the potential upsides of the following courses of action? What are the potential downsides?

OPTION 1: Lee Chan arranges for Lisa to enter group counseling for sexual assault victims. When the other members of the group learn that Lisa continues to be molested, they convince her to move out of the house into her grandmother's home. With trauma counseling, Lisa begins to rebuild her life.

Positive Outcome: Lisa is no longer a victim of her uncle's sexual molestation. She has not damaged the fabric of her family life or caused her uncle to be deported.

Negative Outcome: Lisa not only suffers from intense anger toward her uncle, she fears that he will begin to molest other young female members of the family. She misses her sisters.

Option 2: After several months of counseling, Lisa confronts her uncle and tells him that if he ever touches her again, she will report him to the police. He stops touching her.

Positive Outcome: Lisa feels empowered by the positive outcome. She does not report her uncle to the police and therefore he is not at risk of deportation.

Negative Outcome: Lisa reveals to her uncle during the confrontation that she has a support group of experts that have helped her understand that his behavior constitutes sexual abuse. The uncle takes revenge on her by revealing to the grandfather and head of the family that she has gone outside the family, made false accusations, and has therefore shamed everyone. The grandfather is furious with Lisa.

Ethical Standard 3.3: *Victim assistance providers must refrain from behaviors that communicate victim blame, suspicion regarding victim accounts of the crime, condemnation for past behavior, or other judgmental, antivictim sentiment.*

Carlotta, a victim assistance provider at the police department, often encounters teenage women in the Hispanic community who are at serious risk of violence when they break off with their boyfriends. Usually, she hides these women in shelters until they work out safe, long-term living solutions. Today, Inez, who is only sixteen, was fired upon by someone she believes (but can't prove) was her ex-boyfriend. After a great deal of resistance, Carlotta gets Inez to agree to stay home and out of sight while Carlotta looks for a safe place for her to stay until she can help Inez relocate to another city to live with her aunt. However, all the shelters are full. Carlotta feels extremely frustrated and goes so far as to pressure a shelter manager across town to move a client to a hotel. But before this happens, Carlotta receives a call saying that Inez has been hospitalized for a gunshot wound to the hip that she received while standing in front of a popular club. Carlotta is angry because Inez did not stay home and out of sight and she realizes that she doesn't even want to see her.

Victim assistance providers must avoid doing or saying anything that might communicate suspicion, blame, doubt, or condemnation of the victim's actions or nonactions regarding the crime.

Part 1: Assess case details.

Carlotta has a professional responsibility to support Inez.

Carlotta has a responsibility to respect the policy and procedures of the domestic violence shelters as her partners in the service of victims.

Carlotta is demonstrating symptoms of burnout.

Inez's appearance in front of a popular bar was high-risk behavior.

Inez is a teenager and doesn't like being stuck at home.

Part 2: Separate practical considerations from ethical considerations.

PRACTICAL CONSIDERATIONS	ETHICAL CONSIDERATIONS
Carlotta's reaction to Inez's poor judgment.	3.3 Refrain from victim blaming.
Carlotta's frustration and anger.	1.4 Professional competence.
Safety issues and fear.	3.2 Primary responsibility is the interests of the person served.
Carlotta's overstepping boundaries with shelter advocates.	2.1 Respect for relationships with colleagues and other professionals.

Part 3: What are the potential upsides of the following courses of action? What are the potential downsides?

OPTION 1: Carlotta deals with her anger effectively. While Inez is hospitalized, Carlotta requests an emergency meeting of victim assistance providers in the community to address policies and procedures for housing victims in the shelters.

Positive Outcome: Carlotta realizes that she may have misperceptions about the shelters' ability to meet the needs of victims. Providers agree upon an emergency protocol for high-risk cases so that there is always at least one short-term space in the shelter community for women in extreme danger.

Negative Outcome: Carlotta forgets her strong negative reaction and symptoms that she may be feeling burned out by her job. The next time she is faced with a situation where a victim behaves foolishly, she screams at her.

OPTION 2: Carlotta can't come to terms with her angry feelings toward Inez because of what she views as her reckless behavior. Carlotta asks her agency to assign another advocate to Inez's case.

Positive Outcome: Carlotta recognizes that she is experiencing burnout, and that it would be appropriate for Inez to be referred to another advocate who is more likely in a better mindset to help her. Carlotta takes care to explain kindly and clearly to Inez why she is referring her to another provider.

Negative outcome: The new advocate is not Hispanic, she does not know the community, and Inez does not relate to her. Inez goes home after one night in the shelter and decides that she would rather put up with her ex-boyfriend's behavior than leave her friends for another city.

Ethical Standard 3.4: *Victim assistance providers respect the victim's right to self-determination.*

A neighbor calls the police when Mary's drunken boyfriend chases her through their apartment with a knife, threatening to kill her. Jerry, a community-based victim assistance provider who fulfills the function of advocate for the DA's office, is called upon to meet with Mary after the incident. It is clear to him that while Mary should break up with the boyfriend for safety reasons, the victim is unwilling to leave her home and the financial support he provides. Jerry respects her point of view and does not try to dissuade her. However, an assistant district attorney meets with Mary on a day when Jerry is out of the office. After hearing the story, the ADA is convinced that it is Jerry's professional responsibility to protect Mary by moving her to a safe place, and that the office will be liable if Jerry fails to do so.

Victims have the most informed perspective regarding their personal history, victimization, and risk, and therefore they have ultimate authority over their interests. If the provider's perceptions of what is best for a victim are at odds with that victim's point of view, information can be presented to broaden the victim's perspective. Ultimately, the provider should encourage victims to make their own decisions.

Part 1: Assess case details.

Mary has legitimate financial concerns regarding her home and lack of income.

Jerry faces a conflict of interest in his roles as community-based advocate for Mary and a system-based advocate for the prosecutor's office.

The ADA believes that there are legal considerations concerning liability.

A protection from abuse order that allows both individuals to remain in the home under specific conditions might address the immediate problem of safety.

Part 2: Separate practical considerations from ethical considerations.

PRACTICAL CONSIDERATIONS	ETHICAL CONSIDERATIONS
Disagreement over how to address Mary's safety concerns.	3.4 Right to self-determination.
Role as community-based advocate for Mary and a system-based advocate for the prosecutor's office.	3.6 Avoid conflict of interests.
Financial concerns and loss of home.	3.2 Primary responsibility is the interests of the person served
Disconnect in protocol in the DA's office between victim assistance provider and prosecutor.	1.3 Professional conduct.

Part 3: What are the potential upsides of the following courses of action? What are the potential downsides?

OPTION 1: Jerry sits down with the ADA, discusses principles of advocacy for victims of domestic violence, and convinces the ADA that she must respect Mary's right to stay in her home.

Positive Outcome: Jerry helps Mary with securing a protection from abuse order that allows the boyfriend to remain in the house as long as he does not abuse alcohol, or verbally or physically abuse her. (Mary's state allows for this kind of PFA.) The ADA learns about the importance of victim empowerment and the right to self-determination.

Negative Outcome: The boyfriend gets drunk anyway. He does not respect the court order and assaults Mary.

OPTION 2: Jerry fears that he will lose his job as victim witness advocate if he goes against the ADA and decides to fight the battle over right to self-determination on another occasion. He puts Mary in touch with a colleague at the domestic violence coalition who is better able to support her.

Positive Outcome: Mary seeks counseling at the coalition, develops a safety plan, and joins a support group where she meets several women in abusive relationships who inspire her to change her life.

Negative Outcome: By bending to the pressures of the ADA, Jerry feels that he has lost an opportunity to improve understanding of victims' rights and concerns in the agency. Mary feels disrespected by the prosecutor's office when they insist that she move from her home.

Ethical Standard 3.5: *Victim assistance providers must preserve the confidentiality of information provided by the client or acquired from other sources before, during, and after the course of the professional relationship.*

Sally is a counselor at a homicide survivor group and has a close relationship with Jeffrey Oglesby, whose partner, Sam, was murdered. Sally knows that Jeff is battling a cocaine addiction and has helped him secure drug treatment out of state. Sally believed that Jeffrey had been drug- and alcohol-free since that time, but she recently learned that he was arrested as an uninsured driver after wrecking another person's sports car. The passenger in the car was seriously injured. Jeff passed the breathalyzer test, but the district attorney's office thinks he might have been high on something else. Today, Sally found a message on her voicemail from a prosecutor she has known for years asking her to come in to discuss Jeffrey Oglesby.

Victim assistance providers should preserve confidentiality at all times other than in cases identified as exceptions to the standard, which are listed in chapter 1. A violation of confidentiality can be extremely harmful to the victim; it can also potentially leave the victim assistance provider and/or his or her agency open to legal liability. Information about confidentiality should be provided to the victim at the first meeting or at least at the first available opportunity. In disclosing information regarding confidentiality or in communicating to a victim the fact that certain confidential information may need to be disclosed, the provider should be prepared to address the victim's reaction to this disclosure.

Part 1: Assess case details.

Sally has a professional relationship with Jeffrey through the survivor support group.

They have frequently discussed his addiction problems.

Jeffrey may be a dangerous driver. At the very least it is clear that he was driving without insurance.

Community safety and protection of the right of confidentiality may be competing interests.

There is no statutory protection of confidential privilege for providers in the state where Sally lives and works.

Part 2: Separate practical considerations from ethical considerations.

PRACTICAL CONSIDERATIONS	ETHICAL CONSIDERATIONS
Sally's knowledge of Jeffrey's cocaine addiction.	3.5 Confidentiality of information.
Sally believes that Jeffrey is drug- and alcohol-free.	3.2 Primary responsibility is the interest of the person served.
Sally's relationship with the district attorney's office.	1.3 Professional conduct.
Driving under the influence of illicit drugs is criminal behavior.	1.1 Understand legal responsibilities.

Part 3: What are the potential upsides of the following courses of action? What are the potential downsides?

OPTION 1: Sally asks Jeffrey to meet her for a coffee. She lets him know that the DA has contacted her and that, if subpoenaed, she will have to reveal in court what she knows about his drug addiction. He is adamant that he is drug-free and offers to undergo blood tests to prove it. Sally believes him and promises to be as supportive as possible at the interview with the DA. Sally asks Jeffrey to sign a written consent giving her permission to speak openly with the prosecutor about what she knows about Jeffrey's addiction. He agrees.

Positive Outcome: Sally explains to Jeffrey about the limitations to his right of confidentiality and Jeffrey understands that Sally will make every effort to support him as his advocate during the interview with the DA to avoid being subpoenaed to testify in court. The trusting relationship between the victim service provider and the victim/ survivor is respected.

Negative Outcome: Jeffrey has deceived Sally. He avoids prosecution for the suspected DUI because of the support Sally provided, and he continues abusing drugs.

OPTION 2: Sally meets informally with the DA, and he reveals that Jeffrey has been recently linked to a cocaine dealer in the community and that he is suspected of trafficking in drugs as well as using them. Later, when Sally meets with Jeffrey for coffee, she explains to him that he is in more trouble than he thinks and that if he is abusing substances he should go into a residential treatment program immediately. He agrees to seek treatment.

Positive Outcome: Jeffrey gets the help he needs with his drug addiction. The DA decides not to prosecute and a settlement is reached to cover the injuries of the individual harmed in the car accident.

Negative Outcome: Sally may be aiding and abetting Jeffrey's criminal behavior, the extent of which is unknown and therefore it is unclear if he can be held truly accountable for the harm caused to the community.

Ethical Standard 3.6: *Victim assistance providers must avoid conflicts of interest and disclose any possible conflict to the program or person served, as well as to prospective programs or persons served.*

Veronica, a victim of a violent assault, has several painful injuries that require expensive medication and physical therapy. She is unable to return to her job working in a fast-food restaurant and she has exhausted her eligibility for public assistance. Henry, the police-based victim assistance provider, believes that Veronica is entitled to victim compensation. The officer on the case, however, has connected Veronica with a drug deal gone sour at the time of the assault, which would make her ineligible for compensation. Veronica says her presence near the other crime scene was a coincidence. When Henry visits Veronica at her home, he realizes that the woman is living in abject poverty with her three young children. Henry is tempted to ask his brother, who is a police sergeant, to intervene on her behalf to "clean up" the report so that Veronica could apply for compensation.

Victim assistance providers should not engage in efforts that involve conflicting influences or loyalties that compromise the best interest of the persons or agency served, whether these conflicts are based on professional, personal, family, business, or other relationships. Conflicts of interest can arise as the result of past professional relationships, either within the current position or through some past employment.

Part 1: Assess case details.

> Deteriorating financial stability.
>
> Ineligibility for compensation because of connection to a drug crime.
>
> Boundary issues in question.
>
> Agency conflict of interest.
>
> Adjustment of the police report to help Veronica.

Part 2: Separate practical considerations from ethical considerations.

PRACTICAL CONSIDERATIONS	ETHICAL CONSIDERATIONS
Modifying the police report as a personal favor.	3.6 Avoid conflicts of interests
Victim's dire need for money.	3.2 Primary responsibility is the interest of the person served.
Creation of a precedent for similar (potentially unethical) behavior in other cases.	1.3 Professional conduct.
Henry has breached appropriate boundaries with Veronica.	3.8 Dual relationships.

Part 3: What are the potential upsides of the following courses of action? What are the potential downsides?

OPTION 1: Henry investigates other options to acquire funds to assist Veronica.

Positive Outcome: Henry consults with legal aid, and they offer to represent Veronica in her application to go on disability until she has recovered from her injuries. Once that lengthy process is underway, Henry sets out to find emergency short-term financial assistance for Veronica and discovers a local not-for-profit agency that agrees to help her.

Negative Outcome: Henry has spent so much time concentrating on securing financial assistance for Veronica that his other clients are suffering. Once word gets out, they all want to go on "disability."

OPTION 2: Henry convinces his brother that the police are casting too wide a net when they included Veronica in the report on the drug crime. The officer in charge of the case agrees to remove Veronica's name from the report and Henry fast-tracks the victim compensation payments to Veronica.

Positive Outcome: Veronica receives the funds she needs to improve her poor living conditions while she recovers. Henry is free to dedicate more time to his other clients.

Negative Outcome: Henry is perceived as having inappropriately used his brother's position to advance Veronica's interests. Word gets out that Victim Services is messing with police reports to secure victim compensation. The other officers are grumbling and their relations with the victim advocates are strained.

Ethical Standard 3.7: *Victim assistance providers must terminate a professional relationship with a victim when the victim is not likely to benefit from continued services.*

Chana is a trauma counselor who works with high school teenagers who have been victims of child molestation. Two of her most problematic cases are Tanya and Rosanne, who are best friends and always at risk of suspension from school as chronic troublemakers. Tanya is generally the instigator of the trouble but Rosanne is her loyal follower. Chana feels that her professional relationship with Tanya is ineffective and would like to refer her elsewhere, but she is also aware that she responds negatively to Tanya because of her bad behavior. Rosanne is quite receptive to treatment, however, particularly when she is free of Tanya's negative influences. Yet, Chana fears that she may lose Rosanne's interest and potentially her trust if she terminates the relationship with Tanya. Clearly, the two girls talk about their meetings with Chana and share experiences, which might be the only way Tanya is benefiting, albeit indirectly, from treatment.

When the services offered are no longer relevant to a victim's needs, the victim assistance provider should terminate the professional relationship. The provider should prepare the victim for this eventuality, particularly if the victim is unusually vulnerable and/or derives a great deal of support from their relationship.

Part 1: Assess case details.

Tanya and Rosanne's friendship makes it hard for Chana to reach them independently.

Chana would like to terminate the relationship with Tanya because she believes it is ineffective, but doing may inadvertently sabotage her relationship with Rosanne, which she believes is beneficial.

Chana qualifies her relationships with the two victims based on her perception of the success of the treatments.

Part 2: Separate practical considerations from ethical considerations.

PRACTICAL CONSIDERATIONS	ETHICAL CONSIDERATIONS
The direct services to Tanya appear to be ineffective.	3.7 Termination of professional relationship.
The powerful friendship bond between the youths has negative and positive impact on their lives.	3.2 Primary responsibility is the interests of the persons served.
Judgment of Tanya for her bad behavior.	3.3 Refrain from victim blaming.

Part 3: What are the potential upsides of the following courses of action? What are the potential downsides?

OPTION 1: Chana consults with her supervisor, who agrees to sit in on sessions with both girls for a few weeks, after which time she decides that she will take on Tanya as a client, leaving Rosanne with Chana. They prepare the girls over the next few weeks for the change.

Positive Outcome: Tanya likes the attention that she is receiving from the supervisor and feels quite proud that she has merited a "move up" to Chana's boss. Chana has the opportunity to work more closely with Rosanne on her childhood trauma and over the next few months makes considerable progress.

Negative Outcome: Now that Tanya is under the supervisor's care, Chana inadvertently influences Rosanne to distance herself from her best friend. Rosanne makes negative comments to Tanya, they quarrel, and Rosanne blames Chana for setting her up. Trust in the professional relationship deteriorates.

OPTION 2: Chana takes a wait-and-see approach but the next time the girls are up for a suspension for a serious infraction, Tanya is transferred to an alternative school and the provider-victim relationship with her is automatically terminated.

Positive Outcome: Chana quickly makes a move to find trauma support for Tanya at the new school. Roseanne is free of Tanya's negative influences and more successful in school. Success and validation give her the confidence to address her childhood abuse issues and she moves forward in her life on all fronts.

Negative Outcome: The victim-provider relationship was severed without sensitive preparation, and Tanya is traumatized. Her new school lacks the quality of support and services she was accustomed to. Tanya feels abandoned and her behavior deteriorates even more.

Ethical Standard 3.8: *Victim assistance providers must not engage in personal relationships with persons served which exploit professional trust or which could impair the victim assistance provider's objectivity and professional judgment.*

Jose works for a victim assistance organization where he helps with Spanish-speaking migrant workers who have established permanent residence in the community. One of his clients, Norma, is a victim of domestic violence. In the course of their meetings, Jose has become attracted to Norma and realizes that this attraction affects his ability to serve Norma's best interests effectively and objectively. Norma, on the other hand, is quite dependent on Jose for guidance, revealing that she would never have been able to find the strength to leave her abusive husband if it hadn't been for Jose's support. Furthermore, Jose understands her culture and speaks her language. There is, however, a possibility that Norma will go back with her husband after he finishes the batterers' treatment program, and Jose has to admit that he is jealous. At the same time, he is concerned that referring Norma to another provider will interfere with her progress in the case.

Dual relationships are sometimes difficult to avoid, particularly in small communities. The application of the standard to avoid dual relationships is therefore explored in the context of the potential to cause harm. Whenever there is the potential for loss of objectivity, conflict of interest, or the exploitation of a victim seeking help, the mixing of personal and professional roles is not appropriate. When a provider cannot avoid a personal or business relationship with a client, the provider should seek counsel and supervision from colleagues regarding his or her objectivity regarding the case.

Part 1: Assess case details.

> Norma has just separated from an abusive husband who attends a batterers' treatment program.
>
> Norma would like to return to her husband if and when he has changed his violent behavior.
>
> Jose is the only provider who speaks Spanish and understands Norma's culture.
>
> Norma is dependent on Jose for advice and support.
>
> Jose has romantic feelings for Norma that he fears are affecting his good judgment.

Part 2: Separate practical considerations from ethical considerations.

PRACTICAL CONSIDERATIONS	ETHICAL CONSIDERATIONS
Jose may counsel Norma based on his personal bias rather than her best interests.	3.8 Avoid personal relationships that exploit professional trust.
Norma is dependent on Jose and he is the only culturally competent provider.	3.2 Primary responsibility is the interest of the person served
Jose's romantic feelings compel him to refer Norma to another counselor.	3.7 Termination of professional relationship.

Part 3: What are the potential upsides of the following courses of action? What are the potential downsides?

OPTION 1: Jose reveals his feelings for Norma to his superior as well as his concerns about referring her to another provider. He asks his superior to sit in on their meetings until they can assess his ability to be objective and to determine whether or not her progress might be impeded by a referral.

Positive outcome: Jose's superior expresses her concern over what she considers an unequal relationship but agrees to sit in with him on meetings while she works out an alternative. After she locates a Spanish-speaking counselor at the local clinic, together they take over the provider relationship with Norma.

Negative outcome: Norma misses Jose. When she no longer has Jose as her victim assistance provider, she has difficulty relating to the women replacements. Norma stops coming to her appointments.

OPTION 2: Jose decides to keep his feelings to himself and struggles to remain objective in his dealings with Norma.

Positive Outcome: Norma increasingly values her relationship with Jose whose advice she trusts. Nevertheless, when Norma's husband completes his batterers' treatment program, they move back in together, which is what they both want.

Negative Outcome: Norma checks into the hospital with head injuries from a domestic dispute three weeks later. Jose feels terrible. He tried so hard to remain objective over Norma's marriage that he failed to see the signs of impending danger.

Ethical Standard 3.9: *Victim assistance providers must not discriminate against a victim or another staff member on the basis of race/ethnicity, language, sex/gender, age, sexual orientation, (dis)ability, social class, economic status, education, marital status, religious affiliation, residency, or HIV status.*

Carolyn, who is Caucasian, has a grant to provide assistance to the five culturally and ethnically diverse populations in Los Angeles that have started grassroots homicide survivor groups. Her role as a strategic planner/victim assistance provider is to help them assess their needs as an organization, to assist them in applying for not-for-profit status, and to help them become self-sufficient as support groups for survivors. Carolyn believes that she is color blind—that race and culture are not factors in her job. However, many of the members of the grassroots groups feel that she does not understand them. Over a period of months, they have been increasingly frustrated by her stereotypical views about their cultures. When they ask her to bring in interpreters and members of their own communities to assist her, she replies that the money will be better spent hiring lawyers to secure the not-for-profit status.

A victim assistance provider who is unable to provide services to a victim(s) because of bias or prejudice must inform his or her superiors of the potential bias. Personal bias might be explored through the use of self-inventory tools such as the one presented in chapter 2. If there is any doubt about a provider's ability to offer judgment-free and objective assistance, the provider should seek consultation and/or supervision. In addition, the need for multicultural competency to effectively serve victims of ethnically and culturally diverse communities (described in detail in chapter 2), while not a Consortium standard, is an important factor in the resolution of the above ethical dilemma.

Part 1: Assess case details.

Carolyn is a victim assistance provider who is competent to help groups build stable organizations.

Carolyn believes that she is culturally competent.

Her goal to assist various grassroots organizations has been thwarted by her narrow perception of her job requirements.

Her priorities for the expenditure of grant funds reflect insensitivity to the interests of the persons served.

The groups she is hired to serve feel short-changed.

Part 2: Separate practical considerations from ethical considerations.

PRACTICAL CONSIDERATIONS	ETHICAL CONSIDERATIONS
Carolyn denies that race and culture are relevant factors in her job and ignores the opinions of the multicultural people she serves.	3.9 Do not discriminate.
Carolyn dismisses the survivors' request for people from their community to advise them.	3.2 Primary responsibility is the interests of the person(s) served.
The grassroots groups clearly disagree with Carolyn's approach.	3.4 Right to self-determination.
Insensitive treatment of crime victims.	1.4 Professional competence.

Part 3: What are the potential upsides of the following courses of action? What are the potential downsides?

OPTION 1: Carolyn realizes that she should make a conscious effort to gain more knowledge of the values and beliefs of the various groups with whom she is working, and to understand better how her own racial/ethnic identity impacts her own values and beliefs.

Positive Outcome: Carolyn works to convey more respect and appreciation for the individuals with whom she is working. She attempts to refrain from making assumptions about them and begins to ask them to explain their point of view when they clearly see things differently from her.

Negative Outcome: Carolyn is working with several different cultural/ethnic groups and realizes that she doesn't have time to learn everything she needs to learn to be culturally competent with all of them. She is resigned to doing the best she can in the short time that she has to work with them.

OPTION 2: On advice from colleagues, Carolyn brings in a partner from each community that has formed a homicide survivor group to mediate and clarify areas of concern.

Positive Outcome: The co-victims from the different groups feel that their needs are heard by an understanding voice and that they are more able to realize their goals as an organization.

Negative Outcome: Carolyn observes her organizational process go into reverse and productivity decline rapidly with the introduction of new players who lack the experience and skills required to comprehend the complexity of her strategy. Next time, she will train them before she brings them on board.

 Ethical Standard 3.10: *Victim's assistance providers must furnish opportunities for colleague victim assistance providers to seek appropriate services when traumatized by a criminal event or client interaction.*

Betty and Jo are longtime friends and colleagues at a local domestic violence shelter. They both work the hotline and offer comprehensive on-site assistance to women and children in need of shelter. For the past three years, every Thursday night has been their "sanity" night. They have dinner at a local pub and discuss developments in the shelter. Recently, a client of Jo's was murdered by a husband she refused to leave. Jo is obviously traumatized by the loss. Betty has noticed her expressing anger toward some of the hotline clients who are unwilling to leave their abusive relationships. In the past week, Jo has actually made inappropriate comments regarding what she refers to as their lack of courage in facing the truth of their situations. When Betty hints that her behavior has become a problem, Jo rebuffs her. Betty feels that she should undertake some kind of intervention but doesn't want to do anything to hurt Jo's job security.

In some cases, it may be appropriate for victim assistance providers to offer assistance and feedback to colleagues who have been traumatized by a crime or client interaction. It is common for victim assistance providers to "process" traumatic events or other difficulties experienced in the course of their everyday jobs.

Part 1: Assess case details.

Jo's angry behavior towards clients is harmful, inappropriate, and in violation of ethical standards.

Jo is traumatized by the murder of a client.

Betty is a loyal friend who wants to help Jo without endangering Jo's status at the shelter.

The shelter has no "safety net" organized for staff members suffering from vicarious trauma and compassion fatigue.

Part 2: Separate practical considerations from ethical considerations.

PRACTICAL CONSIDERATIONS	ETHICAL CONSIDERATIONS
Betty wants to help Jo deal with her trauma.	3.1 Referrals for colleagues in need of assistance to cope with trauma.
Jo is conducting herself unprofessionally.	1.3 Professional conduct.
Betty does not want to report Jo's unprofessional behavior to her supervisor.	4.1 Report misconduct.

Part 3: What are the potential upsides of the following courses of action? What are the potential downsides?

OPTION 1: Betty records a few of Jo's angry hotline consultations, plays them back to her over the weekend when she is at home and relaxed, and convinces her to take a short medical leave and undergo an evaluation for stress and burnout.

Positive Outcome: Betty presents Jo with evidence of behavior that she knows is unprofessional and harmful to clients and convinces Jo that she needs to take steps to heal herself of her trauma.

Negative Outcome: Jo feels like she is suffering trauma in the line of duty and resents the fact that the shelter is not there for her, that she has to hide her mental anguish over the loss of a client, and that she has to pay her own mental health bills.

OPTION 2: Betty speaks individually with her colleagues in the shelter about the degree of trauma they experience in their jobs and discovers that on many occasions people have feared for their mental health and their jobs during stressful periods.

Positive Outcome: As a group, they approach their supervisor (Jo included) about creating a safety net for providers experiencing trauma in their jobs. The supervisor develops a response protocol and a list of mental health referrals for the shelter that providers can access anonymously.

Negative Outcome: Without an intervention, Jo lacks the motivation to seek assistance for trauma on her own. Hotline clients begin to complain about her angry behavior over the telephone, and she is moved to a position at the shelter where she has less contact with victims.

Administration and Evaluation

Ethical Standard 4.1: Victim assistance providers must report the conduct of any colleague or other professional (including oneself) to appropriate authorities if that conduct constitutes mistreatment of a person served or brings the profession into dishonor.

Judy is a victim witness advocate who works with Margaret, the director of Victim Services, at the prosecutor's office in a heavily populated midwestern county. Judy is a recent arrival to the office but Margaret has worked there for the past twenty-five years. In fact, Margaret started the program after her daughter was abducted from a local college campus and has almost single-handedly built it into a thriving and heavily supported office of ten full-time professionals. During a complex and arduous trial involving the rape of a young woman from a prominent family, Judy discovers that Margaret is having an affair with the married father of the victim. The victim is Judy's client. The father has been actively involved in the investigation and prosecution strategy since the charges were filed and his daughter adores him. Judy fears the negative impact the affair will have on her client, should it be discovered, and she fears for her job should she confront Margaret.

Providers must report clear violations of ethical standards, including governing boards, funding entities, administrators, and supervisors.

Providers should never knowingly participate in actions that violate ethical standards and are encouraged to self-report violations that require a written report be filed.

Part 1: Assess case details.

The married father of the victim Judy serves is having an affair with Judy's supervisor.

As a rape victim, the daughter is extremely vulnerable.

The father has been an active participant in the strategy for the case.

Margaret is the highly respected founder of the program in which Judy works.

Margaret is in violation of several ethical standards, and if Judy says nothing she will be in violation of at least one standard.

Judy does not want to endanger her job security.

Part 2: Separate practical considerations from ethical considerations.

PRACTICAL CONSIDERATIONS	ETHICAL CONSIDERATIONS
The participants in the unethical conduct are in positions of power and may circumvent Judy's efforts to address this behavior.	4.1 Report misconduct to the appropriate authorities.
Publicizing the affair will cause further trauma to the victim.	3.2 Primary responsibility is the interest of the person served.
Margaret may have undue influence on the victim's father.	3.8 Avoid personal relationships that exploit professional trust.
Margaret is behaving unprofessionally in her relationships with her colleagues, including the victim witness staff and the prosecutors.	1.3 Professional conduct.

Part 3: What are the potential upsides of the following courses of action? What are the potential downsides?

OPTION 1: Judy takes the information about the affair to her supervisor and reports it as an ethical violation.

Positive Outcome: Judy has reported Margaret's unethical conduct to a superior and therefore has discharged her duty to report.

Negative Outcome: The district attorney's office respects the power structure in the community and doesn't want to have problems with the victim's father. No mention of the affair is made to Margaret. The potential for harm to the victim is not addressed.

OPTION 2: Judy tells Margaret that she has observed the depth of personal feelings that she appears to have toward the victim's father without divulging her knowledge of the affair. Judy voices her concerns about the victim's emotional stability, that any little thing could "push her over the edge," and that she doesn't believe that the victim can handle abandonment issues of any kind, such as her father getting involved with Margaret.

Positive Outcome: Margaret pays attention to Judy's concerns and suspends the affair.

Negative Outcome: Judy has not discharged her duty to report Margaret's violations of ethical standards. The victim does not cease to be a traumatized victim at the end of the trial, and will still be vulnerable to the fact that her father is having an affair with a member of her victim support team, should it be discovered.

Conclusion

The NVASC's Ethical Standards presented here offer victim assistance providers a broad set of rules based on the core values of the discipline. Using these as a starting point, providers can build their own organizational code of ethics. However, two points should be clear. First, as a model code, the Consortium standards will change in emphasis when applied to specific victim service organizations according to their community-based or system-based orientation. Second, many ethical dilemmas are experienced as *individual* challenges that must be reflected upon, and resolved in the best way possible. Skill in the resolution of ethical dilemmas can be cultivated with a thorough understanding of the ethical codes, a familiarity with the types of problems that give rise to ethical issues, and practical experience analyzing dilemmas.

General Resources: Understanding and Reflecting on Professional Ethics

Training in professional ethics in victim services is a necessary step to increase personal understanding of the need for ethical standards in the workplace, but implementation requires more. The process of creating a model ethical code in a service provider environment, implementing it, evaluating it, and sustaining it over the long haul involves many steps. Fortunately, resources are available that provide support to individuals who seek to create ethical standards in the workplace, to discuss professional values in their practical applications, and to evaluate the level of ethical compliance at which their organizations can function. Several of these resources are presented below.

1. Self-Awareness Inventory

The following awareness inventory is adapted from *The Trainer's Toolbox: A Resource Guide for Sexual Assault Counselor Training*, published by the Pennsylvania Coalition Against Rape (PCAR) to help individuals contemplate motivations for becoming a victim assistance provider by considering the following questions:

Why did you decide to become a helper?

What was your role in your family as a child?

In general, can you identify what you are feeling? Do you feel comfortable expressing anger, sorrow, or sadness?

What are your feelings about men?

What are your feelings about women?

Have you ever been in treatment? If yes, for what issues?

Are you a survivor of a childhood or adult trauma? If yes, where are you in your process of treatment as a survivor?

How do you feel about working with homosexuals? Minorities? The elderly? Individuals with developmental disabilities?

2. Boundaries: Problem Indicators

The Pennsylvania Coalition Against Rape (PCAR) discusses the importance of setting and maintaining boundaries in *The Trainer's Toolbox: A Resource Guide for Sexual Assault Counselor Training*. It is important for providers to identify ways in which they may overstep professional boundaries while helping victims. To avoid boundary problems with a victim, become aware of the warning signs. The following is a list of feelings/behaviors that are indicators of potential boundary problems:

Frequently allowing sessions with a client to run long

Accepting calls from a client at all hours without setting limits

Overidentifying with a client's happiness, pain, or anger

Feeling angry at or manipulated by a client

Dressing in a manner that the client likes in anticipation of seeing the client

Frequently thinking of the client or feeling compelled to discuss the client with coworkers or others

Showing up at meetings or other places, knowing in advance that the client will be there

Sharing personal details of his or her life that do not directly benefit the client

Feeling afraid of the client

Allowing the client to violate pre-established guidelines of the helping relationship while other clients are not permitted to do so

Wanting to punish a client

The following list represents major violations of boundaries in which a provider's interests take precedent over those of the victim. If a provider acts on any of these feelings, a boundary violation has been committed:

Thinking no one else understands the client

Attending social functions at the client's request[1]

Inviting the client to attend social functions with them

Avoiding terminating a client when termination is appropriate

Placing him- or herself in the role of a therapist

Seeking advice or comfort from a client

Performing tasks for a client that are more appropriate for the client to do, and thereby fostering greater client dependence

Specifically scheduling a client at times when no one else will be in the office

Using the worker-client relationship in any way to fulfill emotional needs

Considering another role with the client, such as friend, employee, coworker, or lover[2]

Complaining to the client about coworkers, supervisor, or working environment

Failing to honor or respect a client's personal space

Touching/hugging a client without his or her expressed consent or when nonverbal communication indicates that he or she does not wish to be touched

Feeling sexually attracted to a client

Feeling sexually aroused in response to a client's description of a sexually abusive incident

Holding a client, not as much out of the client's need to be held but out of the provider's need to hold him or her

Drinking or taking drugs with the client

Having any form of sexualized contact with the client

[1] The decision of whether or not this is a boundary violation depends on intention and the circumstances. In many cultures, visiting a person's home or participating in an event can be part of the trust-building process that allows the provider to be effective.

[2] Again, the decision of whether or nor this is a boundary violation depends on intention and the circumstances. The Domestic Violence/Sexual Assault movement has a history of formerly victimized women becoming involved in victim services, forming friendships with providers, and taking on leadership roles.

3. Evaluation: A Victim Assistance Provider's Ethics Audit

Once an organization or agency has implemented a professional code of ethics, it is important that the program is evaluated for appropriateness, staff buy-in, effectiveness, and compliance. Frederic G. Reamer, a well-known authority on ethics in the field of social work, has prepared an audit to evaluate the impact of newly established professional codes of ethics. The audit can aid practitioners in:

Identifying pertinent ethical issues;

Reviewing and assessing the adequacy of the program with regard to current ethics-related practices;

Modifying practices as needed;

Monitoring the implementation of changes; and

Promoting ethics-related risk management.

An ethics audit should focus on the extent of practitioners' knowledge and understanding of the stated core values of the organization or agency and the known ethics-related risks in the practice setting. The audit should verify the risks and examine current procedures and protocols for handling ethical issues, dilemmas, and decisions.

Before Beginning the Audit

Identify the key topics that appear to be at risk of violation or substandard performance in the workplace. Assign levels of risk to each topic:

- *No risk* would mean that current practices are acceptable.
- *Minimal risk* would mean that current practices are adequate but that minor improvements could be made.
- *Moderate risk* would mean that current practices are problematic and modifications are necessary to minimize risk.
- *High risk* would mean that current practices are seriously flawed and significant modifications are necessary.

Ask some general questions about the organization or agency and the staff:

- What will the auditing committee be looking for in an ethics audit in terms of protocols, recordkeeping, and violations?

- Are procedures in place to identify ethics-related risks and prevent ethics-related complaints?
- What standards are victim assistance providers held to in the workplace?

The ethics audit asks questions and reviews policy, procedures, and performance in the following areas: competency, client rights, confidentiality and privacy, informed consent, conflicts of interest, boundary issues and dual relationships, supervision and training, and ethical decision-making.

Adherence to Professional Ethical Standards

Competency

Note: Refer to NVASC Ethical Standards 1.2, 1.4, and 2.2.

Victim assistance providers should only represent themselves as competent within the boundaries of their education, training, and professional experience. An agency ethics audit should review the following:

Are victim assistance providers in positions that encourage or require them to provide services beyond their range of competency?

Are victim assistance providers using techniques that are new to them without substantive training, practice, and supervision by others competent in the area of expertise?

Is ongoing training available to victim assistance providers for furthering their skills in new areas of victim services?

Are victim assistance providers employing practice approaches and interventions for which there is no generally recognized standard?

Client Rights

Note: All of the NVASC ethical standards are relevant to client rights, but refer specifically to NVASC Ethical Standards 3.1, 3.4, and 3.5.

How frequently and competently are clients informed of their rights? Assess the procedure.

Is there a clearly worded summary of clients' rights that addresses practitioner and agency policy?

A clearly worded summary of clients' rights should cover confidentiality and privacy, release of information, informed consent, access to services, access to records, service plans, service provisions, options for alternative services, right to refuse services, termination of services, and grievance procedures.

Confidentiality and Privacy

Note: Refer to NVASC Ethical Standard 3.5.

1. The ethics audit should review the adequacy of the organization's policy and procedures on:

> Solicitation of private information from clients;

> Disclosure of confidential information to protect clients from self-harm and to protect third parties from harm inflicted by clients;

> Release of harmful information pertaining to alcohol and substance abuse treatment;

> Disclosure of information about deceased clients;

> Release of information to parents and guardians;

> Sharing of confidential information among participants in family and couples; and

> Disclosure of confidential information to media representatives, law enforcement, protective service agencies, and other social service agencies.

2. Policies and procedures should be examined regarding confidentiality, specifically:

> Written and electronic records, and information transmitted to other parties through the use of computers, electronic mail, fax machines, telephone and telephone answering machines, and voice mail;

> Transfer or disposal of client records;

> Protection of client confidentiality in the event of the counselor or advocate's death, disability, or termination of employment;

> Prevention of social discussions of confidential information in public or semipublic areas such as hallways, waiting rooms, elevators, and restaurants; and

> Disclosure of client information for teaching or training purposes.

3. Documentation style and procedures should be reviewed to ensure that:

> Records of factual information are kept diligently.

> Records identify, describe, and assess client circumstances, define the purpose of service, document service goals, plans, and activities, and evaluate the effectiveness of service.

> Records are stored in a locked place.

> Opinions and reflections are not recorded.

Informed Consent

Note: Refer to NVASC Ethical Standard 3.5.

Informed consent is required for release of confidential information, program admission, and service delivery. Does agency policy require:

> Procedures and documents that ensure that coercion and undue influence do not affect a client's decision to consent?

> Verification that the client is mentally capable of providing consent?

> Clear language so that the consent is not blanket but specific to procedures or actions within a definite time frame?

> Communication to clients of their right to refuse or withdraw consent?

> The use of clear and valid consent forms?

> Provision of a consent form in the primary language of the person served?

Conflicts of Interests

Note: Refer to NVASC Ethical Standard 3.6.

Are procedures in place at the agency that alert staff to the potentiality of conflicts of interest?

Boundary Issues and Dual Relationships

Note: Refer to NVASC Ethical Standard 3.8.

An audit should examine the extent to which victim assistance providers have been provided with clear criteria to help them maintain proper boundaries with clients with regard to:

Sexual relationships with current and former clients;

Friendships with clients, encounters with clients in public settings, physical contacts, and gifts to and from clients;

Delivery of service to two or more people who have a relationship with each other as couples or family members;

Attending client social or lifecycle events; and

Self-disclosure to clients.

Supervision and Training

Note: Refer to NVASC Ethical Standards 2.2 and 4.1.

Agency supervisors generally have oversight responsibilities for ethical breaches by those under their supervision. Furthermore, they may be held responsible or partially responsible for actions or inactions in which they are involved indirectly as supervisor. Therefore:

Supervisors should be able to identify and respond to supervisee errors in all phases of client contact.

Supervisors should encourage and facilitate the skill and knowledge development of the organization staff.

Supervisors should be able to determine when specialized expertise is needed for appropriate care for a client and ensure that appropriate referrals are made.

Supervisors should meet regularly with supervisees; review and approve supervisee records, decisions, and actions; and provide adequate coverage in the supervisee's absence.

The ethics audit should also review agency training to determine if staff understand and are able to practice the professional code of ethics to which the agency has ascribed. The ethics training should include:

Discussion and review of issues related to relevant practice skills, major areas of risk, and relevant state and local statutes that affect ethical decision-making; and

Assessment tools, intervention techniques, and evaluation methods.

Ethical Decision-Making

An ethics audit should assess victim assistance providers' familiarity with the kinds of ethical dilemmas that may occur in the fulfillment of their professional duties, and whether victim assistance providers have acquired skills that assist them in thinking through dilemmas in a manner consistent with the values and standards set forth by the professional code of ethics. The audit should determine if the victim assistance provider can apply decision-making protocols. Some examples of ethical dilemmas might include:

> The enforcement of client's rights that may result in a situation that is harmful for the client, for example, a battered woman's self-determination versus her engagement in behavior that increases her vulnerability.

> Choices about the allocation of limited agency resources, for example, budgeting for increases in volunteer training when staff would benefit from compassion fatigue counseling.

> Choices on managing agency misconduct when exposure will tarnish its reputation in the community.

Making Constructive Use of an Ethics Audit

Individual practitioners, administrators and committees formed within institutions to address ethical oversights can follow several steps:

> Establish priorities among the areas of concern based on degree of risk involved and available resources.

> Articulate specific measures that need to be taken to address the problem areas.

> Identify staff that will be responsible for fulfilling the tasks needed to remedy problem areas.

> Create a timetable for completion of each task.

> Monitor the implementation of the assigned tasks.

> Evaluate the completed tasks for efficacy in dealing with the problem area.

4. Recommendation for Resolution of Interagency Conflicts

As part of their Code of Ethics, the Colorado Victim Services 2000 Program has developed recommendations in four areas for use by service providers in the resolution of interagency conflicts:

1. *Establishing protocols for identifying conflicts and how parties will be involved in resolution.* Victim assistance agencies should develop a process for dealing with intra- and interagency conflicts. Generally speaking, coworkers in the same agency who are involved in a conflict should confront each other directly. Because the resolution of interagency conflicts may have political implications, consult with a supervisor or director before taking action to resolve a problem. If the conflict involves coworkers at different levels in the agency power structure, measures should be taken to equalize the power by using a mediator. It is important that resolution take place at the level on which the conflict occurs and should include everyone involved in the conflict even if the situation is being addressed at the supervisor/director level. Solutions to conflicts should always be developed with the best interests of the victim in mind.

2. *Preparations for conflict resolution session.* Before attempting resolution, schedule the session, identify the participants, and define the nature of the conflict. Assess the cultural considerations relevant to the situation and take measures to address them. Decide whether or not an unbiased party with an objective viewpoint should facilitate the session.

3. *Procedures during conflict resolution session.* Ask all parties participating in the session to agree to maintain the confidentiality of the discussion. Allow everyone the opportunity to express their view of the conflict and how it has impacted them or their client. Ask the participants to brainstorm for creative solutions and remind them to be respectful of each other's ideas. Strive for a win-win solution that serves both the victim and the participating individuals, and honors the identity, mission, and scope of the agencies. Ask the parties to agree on a solution they can commit to and implement in a reasonable time frame. Make sure everyone understands in detail what he or she is agreeing to. Put the agreement in writing in clear and succinct language, so that everyone can communicate it accurately to clients and colleagues.

4. *Post-session follow-up.* Ask all participating parties to report the agreed-upon solution to their agencies and implement changes. At the end of the agreed-upon time frame, ask everyone to evaluate the outcome and determine whether the conflict has been resolved to the mutual satisfaction of all parties or whether further steps are needed. Any parties who do not fulfill their part of the agreement should be held accountable. If intra-personal conflicts arise that cannot be addressed

by the conflict resolution procedure, the agencies should commit to providing support to the individuals involved in resolving their issues.

5. The Conflict Resolution Process

The mission of the Victim Services Network (VSN) of Denver and Denver County, Colorado, is to create a model network of services that is innovative, specialized, seamless, and integrated, for all crime victims, especially the unserved and the underserved. In December 2004, VSN drafted a conflict resolution process to address inter- and intra-agency conflicts among victim service providers. The conflict resolution process was created in recognition that in any collaborative body conflicts will arise and that the network should strive to provide an environment that ensures that members feel comfortable acknowledging, discussing and problem solving around the issues in conflict. Two guiding values have been prominent in the creation of the conflict resolution policy. The first is to commit to a victim-centered process, and the second is to assume good intent of all VSN members.

Philosophy of Conflict Resolution

VSN adapted a mode of communication for conflict resolution based on a model of direct communication between the parties in conflict. However, VSN recognizes that direct communication is not always the most effective model of conflict resolution for all situations. Though direct communication is encouraged in order to place the responsibility of problem solving on the two parties involved, not all cultures would use this model and in fact, direct communication may be viewed as disrespectful in some cultures. Furthermore, depending on the conflict, direct communication does not take into account power imbalances. This process recognizes these difficulties with the direct communication model and allows for parties to construct other avenues for approaching and facilitating conflict resolution.

Purpose of the Conflict Resolution Process

The purpose of the conflict resolution process is to provide an avenue to listen to disputes or conflicts that impact the quality of victim services and to assist the parties in crafting resolutions.

A conflict should be brought to this process when:

> Disputes and conflicts have an impact on the network of services. If the issue cannot be defined as impacting services, then it will not be heard by the Conflict Resolution Committee (CRC).

> The CRC is "the last resort" for issues. An issue should be brought to the committee after all possible steps have been taken to resolve the issue, for example, supervisors/directors have attempted to deal with the issue, intra-agency conflict resolution protocols have been put into practice, and so on.

Conflict Resolution Committee Structure

A committee should be composed of three members of the VSN and two alternate positions in cases of conflict of interests. (See chapters 2 and 5 for information on conflicts of interest.) The CRC should include representation from both the system- and community-based service providers that include heads of agencies/organizations and staff. Members should be nominated by heads of organizations and approved by a simple majority vote of the membership.

In addition, a CRC member should act as lead contact, with committee terms of one year and no consecutive terms. Issues should be brought to the lead contact or to the director of the VSN.

Conflict Resolution Process

Initiating the Process

Point of Entry: The process begins when one party contacts the lead CRC member or VSN staff member because of a conflict.

Provision of Background Information: The party presents the history of the issue and the steps taken to resolve the issue. The CRC needs to know the following information:

- The specific issue
- The history
- Recent attempts to address the issue
- If it is a personal conflict or if it involves services (the issue could be a personality conflict that affects services or just a personality conflict).

- If the party can interact on behalf of the victim personally and professionally

Note: It is not within the scope of the CRC to work with a victim to create a resolution to a conflict.

The Process

The initiating party and the CRC lead member decide together if there is enough information to proceed and that every attempt has been made to resolve the issue prior to approaching the committee.

The CRC lead member will first contact and update the committee to notify them of a conflict. The CRC lead member will then notify the secondary party to come to a committee meeting. If the second party refuses to meet with the CRC to discuss the issue, then the CRC will take the issue to the VSN. If timing does not allow a prompt response from the VSN, then the issue will be taken to the VSN Executive Committee. Refusal to participate in the process can lead to the second party being asked to leave VSN.

The CRC will meet with a representative from each agency. In order to address power imbalance and to develop familiarity and consistency with the conflict resolution process each VSN member will have one representative from the agency appointed to deal with the conflict resolution process. This person should have decision-making authority. In addition, each party may bring one person who is directly involved with the issue and can assist in clarifying program priorities and services.

The Role of the CRC

The CRC acts as the objective facilitator. The CRC is responsible for working with the two parties to

Establish ground rules;

Create an outline of the steps to be taken by both parties to resolve the conflict and improve service delivery; and

Record summarization of the resolution to be given to all parties.

The final solution should be focused on the network of services and be victim-centered. By no means are the CRC committee members professional mediators. Their role is to listen and to assist in crafting a resolution. If parties feel that the situation requires professional mediation, the CRC involvement in the process should be terminated.

However, the CRC should request information about the outcome of any professional mediation that affects the network.

Improving services for crime victims is an on-going process that requires commitment and time. Consequently, the CRC may request a follow-up meeting to check on progress. If there is improvement in services then the CRC may request future meetings to reexamine the issue and the proposed resolution.

Memorandum of Understanding (MOU)

As part of the agreement among victim service agencies and organizations in Denver and Denver County, members signed a memorandum of understanding that confirmed their willingness to participate in the Conflict Resolution Process. The MOU on the facing page describes the spirit in which parties agree to enter into the process.

References

Colorado Victim Services 2000 (Colorado VS2000). Victim Service Provider Code of Ethics. <http://www.vs2000.org/denver/english/ttac/train/trng.htm>

Colorado Victim Services 2004. *Conflict Resolution Process.* Denver: *Victim Services Network.*

Pennsylvania Coalition Against Rape. 2000. *The Trainer's Toolbox: A Resource Guide for Sexual Assault Counselor Training.* Harrisburg: Pennsylvania Department of Public Welfare.

Reamer, F. July 2000. "The Social Work Ethics Audit: A Risk Management Strategy." *Social Work* 45(4):353–66. Copyright 2000, National Association of Social Workers, Inc., Social Work.

Memorandum of Understanding Conflict Resolution Process

We, the members of the Victim Services Network, reaffirm the original mission of the collaboration:

...to create a model network of services for all crime victims, especially the unserved and the underserved, which is innovative, specialized, seamless and integrated.

As a collaborative body the group recognizes that conflict will arise and that the network will strive to provide an environment that ensures that members feel comfortable acknowledging, discussing and problem solving around these issues.

In the spirit of continuing to enhance services, this process was developed with two guiding values in creating the conflict resolution policy. The first is to commit to a victim-centered process, and the second is to assume good intent of all VSN members.

We will continue to work toward this mission by:

1. Developing mutual trust and respect among victim service agencies, allied professionals, and the community.

2. Creating a structure and environment where both policy and case specific conflicts can be resolved.

3. Realizing that the goal of this process is to create a vehicle for dealing with conflict in a manner that will continue to enhance services to crime victims.

Index

VALOR

The Victims' Assistance Legal Organization, Inc. (VALOR), a 501(c)(3) not-for-profit corporation, was established in 1979 by the late Frank Carrington, one of the early proponents of victims' rights. It was his intention that the organization provide leadership on issues related to the rights of crime victims in America. Carrington has often been referred to as the "father of the crime victims' rights movement in America," and VALOR has consistently pursued the vision that was his trademark.

VALOR is dedicated to enhancing victims' rights in the civil, criminal, and juvenile justice systems and to advancing victims' rights through public policy efforts on the federal, state, and local levels. Through the promotion of public education and awareness about the rights and needs of crime victims, the organization works to improve services for victims to assist in their emotional, financial, and physical recovery. VALOR accomplishes its mission through support from private and corporate foundations, government grants, and individual contributions. For more information, visit www.valor-national.org.

Sidran Institute

Sidran Institute is a 501(c)(3) nonprofit organization of international scope that helps people understand, treat, and recover from the effects of victimization, trauma, and dissociative conditions. In addition to service providers, Sidran's constituents include family members and victims of all types of traumatic experiences, including rape, child abuse and neglect, domestic violence, assault, murder of a loved one, and/or crime related to substance use. Building on a philosophy of "education through collaboration," Sidran convenes survivors, professionals, and lay support providers to develop programs and products to address the practical, emotional, and health needs of trauma survivors.

Sidran was founded in 1986 and named for Kate Sidran, whose donation enabled its launch and whose bequest continues to support approximately 10 percent of the organization's annual operations. Individual contributions as well as grants enable the work. For more information, visit www.sidran.org.

Melissa Hook is the deputy executive director of the Victims' Assistance Legal Organization and a national crime victim advocate.

CPSIA information can be obtained
at www.ICGtesting.com
Printed in the USA
LVHW08s0246070718
582982LV00001BA/1/P